FERRIES & PLEASURE
STEAMERS OF
THE BRITISH ISLES

A wonderfully timeless scene showing the Caledonian MacBrayne ferry *Claymore* loading at Port Askaig, Islay on 23rd May 1992.
Joe McKendrick

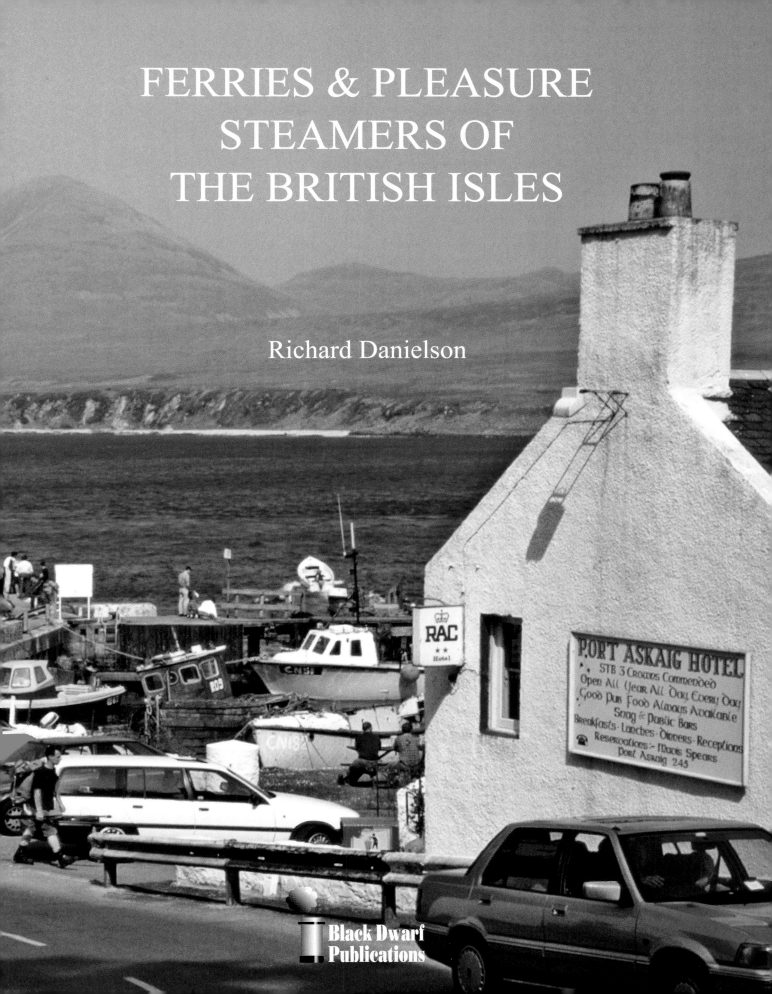

FERRIES & PLEASURE STEAMERS OF THE BRITISH ISLES

Richard Danielson

Black Dwarf
Publications

The paddle steamer *Caledonia* (1934) at Tarbert, Loch Fyne in late April 1969. She had been chartered by David MacBrayne for their daily Royal Mail service from Gourock due to the absence of the usual vessel *Lochfyne*, which was standing in for the broken down *Lochnevis* on the Islay run. The writer and his wife had a great affection for *Caledonia* having sailed on her during their honeymoon, a few days before this photograph was taken. Their route from Gourock took them to Craigendoran where the ship grounded gently and spent a while, paddles thrashing meaninglessly, until she slipped back off the mud and the voyage proceeded. The ship had been built with the open sea Ardrossan to Arran winter route firmly in mind and so met the scantlings requirements of a Class IIA passenger ship carrying 600 passengers in winter. In summer, in calmer waters, she could accommodate more than twice this number. Happy days!
Joe McKendrick

© Black Dwarf Publications & Richard Danielson 2019
Designed by Richard Danielson
British Library Cataloguing-in-Publication Data. A catalogue record for this book is available from the British Library
ISBN: 978190359925 9

BLACK DWARF PUBLICATIONS
Unit 144B, Harbour Road Trading Estate, Lydney, Gloucestershire GL15 4EJ
www.lightmoor.co.uk / info@lightmoor.co.uk
Black Dwarf Publications is an imprint of Black Dwarf Lightmoor Publications Ltd
Printed in Poland
www.lfbookservices.co.uk

CONTENTS

Introduction 6

Chapter 1   Photographed in and around the Firth of Clyde, the Western,
             Outer and Northern Isles 8

Chapter 2   Photographed in and around the Irish Sea, the Isle of Man,
             the North West and Wales 40

Chapter 3   Photographed in and around Britain's South West, the South Coast and
             the Channel Isles 88

Chapter 4   Photographed in and around the River Thames, England's East Coast and
             Cruising BR Style much further afield 136

Chapter 5   A few words of appreciation about some of our photographers who, sadly, are no
             longer with us and thanks and acknowledgements 152

Index 158

This picturesque scene at Oban in October 1972 shows *Columba* alongside the North Pier and *Loch Arkaig*, which at the time was relieving *Loch Toscaig*, starting out on her run to Lismore, a journey taking her about an hour. She was timber-built in 1942 by J. Bolson & Sons Poole and was given new Bergius engines and an aluminium and steel superstructure when converted for passenger carrying in 1959/60. She was a tough little vessel having originally been an inshore minesweeper in World War 2, but in MacBrayne's service with a Class IIA passenger certificate while based at Mallaig, she often ventured well out into open water on voyages of several hours duration around the Small Isles.

Joe McKendrick

INTRODUCTION

The main aim of this album is to showcase the work of the photographers whose fine studies of the ships we love are featured in this book. Large collections of their original photographic images and material they collected are now under my ownership and care, and in due course all the images will have been digitally saved and restored electronically for future generations to enjoy.

I have great belief in the notion that 'One picture is worth a thousand words'.

Choosing some 260 or more photographic images from collections in my care totalling many thousands, plus, where the context required them, a few of my own photographs and some from my personal collection, is necessarily subjective and what appeals to some, may be anathema to others. I do hope my selections meet with approval and that there is plenty here for all tastes and enough of any one genre to be worthwhile.

Most of the images are appearing in print for the first time and I, like many other photographers, take several exposures of basically the same view to enable their individual reproduction. A few, that are really special, have been seen before many years ago.

The range of photographs covers about a century of small passenger ship operations and the reader will readily recognise the names of the photographers whose pictures appear here. Sadly, some of them are no longer with us but through compilations like this, their legacy lives on. Towards the back of the book, readers will find a few words of appreciation I have written about each of them.

Others, thankfully, are still very much alive and all of the photographers past and present and those with whom the writer remains happily in contact, may rightly be looked upon as masters of the art of ship photography.

Rather than fill the captions with irrelevant contractions like Co., Ltd, just for the sake of being legally and grammatically correct, for the most part I have used the easily recognisable form of company names such as MacBrayne's, Cosens, Steam Packet and Red Funnel, etc.

The Isle of Man has been our home for nearly fifty years – most of our working lives and now into retirement – and I have been heartened to know how popular our island has been amongst ship photographers generally. Some, from Scotland especially, looked upon the Isle of Man as a place akin to the Southern Hebrides and many came here time after time.

I would like to extend my thanks to Peter Sunderland, an extraordinarily good, widely-travelled and knowledgeable photographer, whose extensive collection of original maritime and railway material I digitised, restored and had printed a few years ago. Peter has single-handedly created a collection of great national importance and I am grateful to him for allowing me complete freedom of access to use his fine photography in my books.

Iain Quinn, who is a well-known specialist in Clyde steamer circles and a national lecturer on the subject, recently passed to me a collection of evocative black and white negatives taken by Fred Plant in his travels beyond Scottish waters. Fred Plant handed them down to Stuart Rankin and he in turn to Robin Boyd, who passed them to Iain Quinn. Some of these rare images are featured here too. Iain sought nothing in exchange and I wish to thank him for entrusting this fine collection to me.

A long-standing and expert shipping friend of mine, Michael Walker of Hest Bank, Lancaster, sadly passed away recently. Some years previously, Mike and I arranged a mutually good exchange of maritime materials, which happily brought into my ownership and care many superb original negatives taken by two photographic heavyweights, namely Henry (H.M.) Rea and W. Paul Clegg. Some of them appear in this book.

Coastal shipping experts Keith Abraham, Keith Adams and Don Jones have provided unfettered access to their vast store of knowledge, commentary and fine photography, without which some of this would not have been possible.

My critical readers Malcolm McRonald and John Newth are both well-known and trusted maritime writers and historians, and I am very grateful to them for carrying out this essential, painstaking task.

I am obliged to Neil Parkhouse of Black Dwarf Lightmoor Publications Ltd and to graphic designer Ade Haines at Artytype in Lydney for so ably helping me to bring this book to fruition, thus keeping the memory of the ships and the photographers alive for future generations, and to Tony Davies for getting me started with the latest Quark 2017 software.

The chain of custody of old photographic material continues but seeking out new homes for such material, without condemning it to dusty archive shelves often closed to the public eye, is a huge issue about which I worry a lot.

I am privileged to have known many ship photographers personally and to be able to share in the custody of their fine photographic work and to help to see it published. I thank them for the enjoyment their skill and dedication will bring to us for many years to come.

This book is a tribute to them all.

Richard Danielson
Isle of Man

20 November 2018

Penzance, Cornwall, has been a harbour and dry-dock facility the writer and members of his family have been visiting for fifty years. Early in those days the service to the Scilly Islands was maintained by *Scillonian* (2) dating from 1956. At the time, Penzance was a very busy port for Trinity House whose vessels also regularly frequented Holman's Dry Dock (which is now operated by the Isles of Scilly Steamship Company). Likewise, in P.&A.Campbell's time, *Balmoral* welcomed the writer and his father-in-law from his village shop and post office at St. Mabyn, every year she was laid up there. *Scillonian's* successor in 1977 was *Scillonian III* and she provided the writer and his wife a very lively crossing to St. Mary's and back on 9th September 2011. The following day with the sea still running there was torrential rain interspersed with bright sunlight – the ideal formula for a brilliant rainbow through which *Scillonian III* sailed as she swung in to berth at the Lighthouse Pier, Penzance. Now, at the age of over 40 years, the successor for *Scillonian III* is being actively discussed.

Richard Danielson

MacBrayne's *Lochfyne* resting at Tarbert, Loch Fyne, during her daily Royal Mail run from Gourock to Ardrishaig and back. This route had been the summer preserve of the famous *Saint Columba* (1912 ex-*Queen Alexandra* – 1936) until 1958, after which her certificates expired and she was scrapped. *Saint Columba* had a Class V smooth water passenger certificate for 1,800. The smaller capacity and more efficient *Lochfyne* (1931) having been built as the winter vessel on this route (latterly only as far as Tarbert with a connecting bus service taking passengers further north) took over the service all year round. 1969 was the final year for this picturesque mail route with the coming of the Scottish Transport Group.

Joe McKendrick

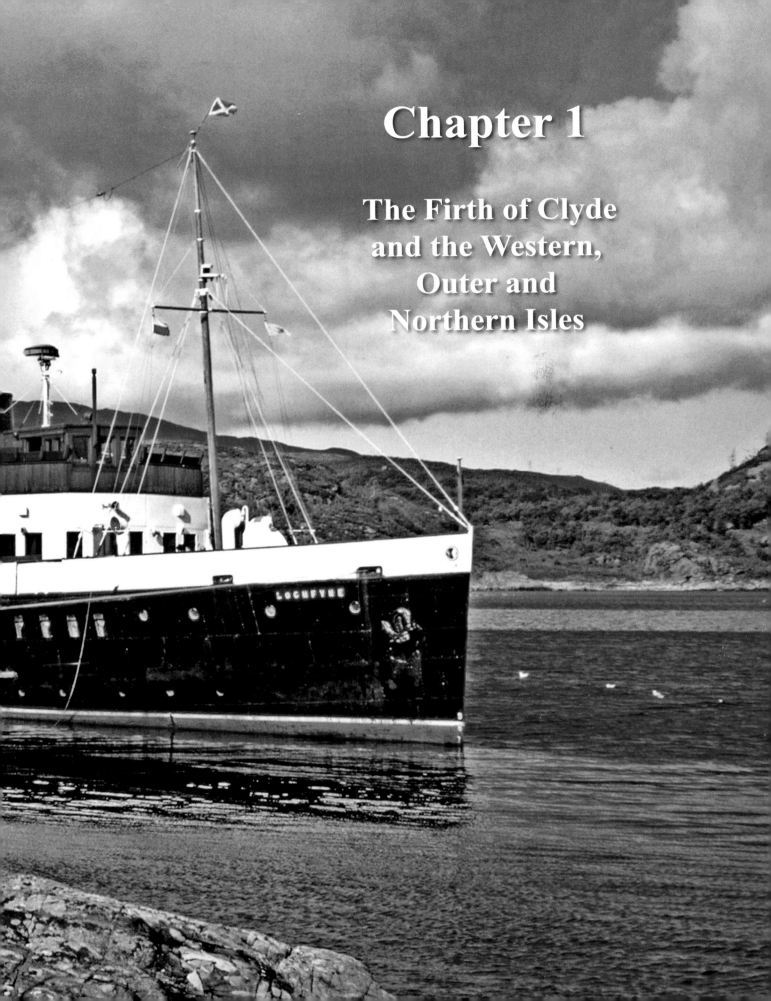

Chapter 1

The Firth of Clyde and the Western, Outer and Northern Isles

The incomparable *Duchess of Hamilton* (1932) seen here off Keppel Pier, Millport, Cumbrae in September 1970, her final month of commercial sailing before being retired and later sold. This scene records the Clyde River Steamer Club (CRSC) charter from Ayr to Ardrishaig on 5th September 1970 and that the large number of passengers on the pier are probably awaiting the arrival of *Queen Mary II* to take them on to Largs, Dunoon and Gourock while the 'Duchess' returned to Ayr.

Joe McKendrick

Perfectly reflected in the smooth waters of the River Clyde, *Shanklin* (1951) was acquired by the 'Waverley Organisation' to be the support vessel for the preserved paddle steamer. This photograph dates from the end of November 1980, when the ship had been newly brought up to Stobcross Quay, Glasgow (via Kyles of Bute and Helensburgh) from Portsmouth where she had operated the British Railways (B.R.) passenger ferry service to the Isle of Wight. Ancillary to her main duties she tendered liners anchored-off in Cowes Roads, and ran summer excursions and trips to see the liners in Southampton Docks.

Joe McKendrick

This splendid shot at Bridge Wharf, Glasgow was taken in summer of 1969. *Duchess of Hamilton* is enjoying a heave-off by two of the Clyde Navigation Trust's (then only recently merged into the Clyde Port Authority) harbour launches, which look to be pulling very hard to achieve the necessary effect. Without this tow, the manoeuvre could be accomplished by running a very long mooring line from the port bow to a quayside bollard well back beyond the stern and literally steaming against it with the rudder hard over. Immediately the turn had been completed, the 'Duchess' tied up again at Bridge Wharf, port side to, ready to receive her passengers and for the subsequent departure down river, taking her under the Kingston Bridge then under construction, and probably on as far as Tighnabruaich – Kyles of Bute.

Joe McKendrick

Early in the 1969 season, *Maid of Ashton* (1953) is seen leaving the James Watt Dock, Greenock. Her forward observation lounge windows are covered giving some rough weather protection. She and her three sisters had Class IV passenger certificates (smooth and partially smooth waters) and worked extensively in the Upper Firth on the cross-river sailings and odd excursions but at that time, were not permitted to operate to Arran and beyond. Nowadays named *Hispaniola*, she remains berthed on the Thames Embankment working in the hospitality industry.   *Joe McKendrick*

The new ship for the Ullapool – Stornoway service was the Norwegian-built *Suilven*. She arrived at Gourock on 19th August 1974, where she is seen in this image, direct from Norway. After storing and familiarisation, a week later she was on her way north paying a courtesy visit into Oban on her way to Stornoway. Built for the relatively calm waters of Oslofjord and bought on the stocks by Caledonian MacBrayne, she had no stabilisers. No doubt much to the relief of her passengers, they were added some years later as the Minch can be a notoriously wild stretch of sea.   *Ken Angus*

In early 1970 *Clansman*, seen here at Dunoon, was chartered by the Caledonian Steam Packet Company whose livery she is wearing, to operate their Gourock to Dunoon passenger and car ferry service while new tonnage was awaited. Passengers must have found her very large and luxurious compared with the previous generation 'Maids' and the early 'ABC' car ferries. Built in 1964, *Clansman,* together with sister ships *Columba* and *Hebrides,* was originally owned by the Secretary of State for Scotland and operated by David MacBrayne.

Ken Angus

By the time this fine photograph of *Queen Mary* (1933) was taken showing her at Largs in June 1976, she had just one more season of active service ahead of her. Then, after many years moored on the Thames in the catering and hospitality business, she finally retired to Tilbury where, having been virtually abandoned, but for the unstinting efforts of well-wishers she would have met her end. Against all the odds The Friends of TS Queen Mary secured her future and they have a long-term berth for her in Glasgow, where she now resides and is undergoing sympathetic restoration.

Joe McKendrick

(Above) *Marchioness of Lorne* (1935) seen on 20th June 1952, was best known as the Holy Loch ship. Lying overnight at Kilmun and making calls at Ardnadam, Strone, Blairmore, Kilcreggan, Princes Pier, and Gourock she became a firm favourite with regulars, despite her slow 12-knot speed. Later she served Millport from Largs. The diesel-electric paddler *Talisman* took over the Millport service from June 1954 and with the new diesel 'Maids' now firmly in service too, life was short for *Marchioness of Lorne*. She was scrapped at Port Glasgow in 1955.   *Richard Danielson Collection*

(Opposite top right) *Ashton* (seen arriving at Largs on 8th July 1961) and her sister, *Leven* were both built in 1938 by Wm Denny & Bros, Dumbarton for the Empire Exhibition in Glasgow, and specifically to operate trips designed to showcase the work of the Clyde shipyards. After service in the Second World War they became associated with local services in the Upper Firth and notably on the Largs-Millport service. In they end, they were too small for anything useful being certificated for just 72 passengers so they were sold out of service in 1965. Both remain in different ownership to this day with *Ashton* running successfully as *Wyre Lady* and *Leven* now named *Bristol Queen* but presently laid up under restoration.   *Richard Danielson Collection*

(Opposite top left and bottom) *Countess of Breadalbane* (1936) at Gourock in mid-April 1969, during the writer's honeymoon, some of which was spent at Largs in the much-missed Marine and Curlinghall Hotel. Originally built for service on Loch Awe, as may be seen she had large rectangular windows in her hull which were plated over and made into portholes for service on the Clyde from 1952. After she was finally sold out of the Caledonian Steam Packet fleet in 1971, she saw further service on the Clyde as *Countess of Kempock* and at Oban and Iona where she ran some excursions which must have proved very boisterous on all but the calmest days. 1982 saw her moved to Loch Lomond for the saddest part of her career. Renamed *Countess Fiona* she was not a great success. She changed hands several times and ultimately was withdrawn, abandoned and broken up by a mechanical digger in 1999. A poor end to a fine ship, which was a firm favourite of the writer.   *Richard Danielson*

Maid of Argyll (1953) attempting to berth at Largs in very rough seas, probably on 15th October 1969, when severe gales lashed the Firth of Clyde causing Wemyss Bay, Dunoon and Innellan piers all to be closed for part of the afternoon and evening. The Rothesay sailings were diverted from Wemyss Bay to Gourock and the other routes struggled on as best they could.   *Joe McKendrick*

Maid of Cumbrae (1953), like the other three vessels of her class *(Maid of Ashton, Maid of Argyll* and *Maid of Skelmorlie)* was built for carrying passengers only on all the routes in the Upper Firth and for excursions. With *Arran* still working the Islay routes from West Loch Tarbert, in 1972 *Maid of Cumbrae* was sent to Barclay, Curle's Elderslie shipyard for conversion to a small, but nonetheless very useful, car ferry able to carry about fifteen cars. Here she is in her first summer operating as a car ferry.   *Joe McKendrick*

This is Rothesay Bay in glorious afternoon sunshine in September 1971, with *Maid of Skelmorlie* rounding to, ready to come alongside. A seaman is already on the foredeck with his bow rope ready to be heaved ashore and a handful of passengers are visible on the upper deck ready to disembark.

Joe McKendrick

(Above) At the beginning of 1970, when the car ferry revolution finally caught up with Islay, Jura and Gigha, deep in MacBrayne territory, *Arran* (1953) a Caledonian Steam Packet car ferry, was the vessel chosen to replace MacBrayne's *Lochiel* (1939). The service ran from West Loch Tarbert where the ship became based. This scene shows *Arran* newly resplendent in MacBrayne livery in March 1970 at that location, where she is taking on fuel oil from a road tanker on the pier. *Joe McKendrick*

(Opposite top) Sister ship of *Arran* and *Cowal*, *Bute* (1954) is at Wemyss Bay on 17th July 1972, from where she and *Cowal* provided the service to Rothesay. *Ken Angus*

(Opposite bottom) The car ferry *Cowal* (1954), on 24th March 1973, looking fresh from overhaul at Scotts', Garvel Graving Dock, Greenock making a smart departure from Gourock where she was relieving *Glen Sannox* on the run to Dunoon. *Ken Angus*

(Above) Seen early in her career in the 'Waverley Organisation' on 20th May 1987, *Balmoral* is sailing down the River Clyde beneath the Erskine Bridge. In the top right of the image is the slipway for the old cross-river chain ferry which the new bridge rendered redundant in 1971. *Joe McKendrick*

(Opposite top) This is Dunoon on 26th August 1978, showing Highland Mary Campbell's famous statue and *Arran* coming alongside. In 1972 she had been sent to Barclay, Curle's Elderslie shipyard to be altered to facilitate vehicle end-loading onto a linkspan and in this condition she is shown here. *Ken Angus*

(Opposite bottom) The paddle steamer *Waverley* making smoke on 12th September 1971 – at the time still very much part of the Caledonian Steam Packet fleet – and about to berth at Dunoon with a good complement of passengers. Her stumpy foremast resulted from being blown against the pier at Arrochar on 15th July 1971, causing strain on the forestay which in turn brought down the top half of her foremast – and a long section of deck rail was left behind at the pier too. *Ken Angus*

(Above) Western Ferries' crossing from McInroy's Point (near Gourock) and Hunter's Quay on the Cowal Peninsula can be quite exposed to prevailing winds and big seas. Here we see *Sound of Sleat* (Hardinxveld, Netherlands, 1961) tackling a south westerly gale in January 1991, as she crosses to Hunters Quay.

Joe McKendrick

(Above right) On 9th June 1991, the colourfully dressed *Saturn* operated a charter sailing from King George V Dock, Glasgow, to Gourock and Rothesay. *Joe McKendrick*

(Right) Two exiles from the South. *New Roseland* of Helensburgh Seaways (ex-*Royal Jubilee*, Cook, Welton & Gemell, Beverley, Hull, 1935) late of Bridlington, River Fal and the Thames) and *Kenilworth* (ex-*Hotspur II*, Rowhedge Ironworks, 1936) the former Southampton - Hythe ferry, at Helensburgh.

Joe McKendrick

(Below) Queens Dock Glasgow in April 1969 and the majestic *King George V* looking resplendent in the welcome, if wintry, sunshine. A far cry from how she appeared a few days earlier when the writer and his wife visited the ship in a blinding snowstorm whilst on their honeymoon. This would be the final winter lay-up in the Queens Dock, which was permanently closed shortly thereafter and subsequently redeveloped to include the Scottish Exhibition & Conference Centre, the Armadillo and the Crowne Plaza Hotel. *Joe McKendrick*

Jeanie Deans (1931) approaching Dunoon on the return leg of her journey on a late summer afternoon in the early 1950s and about to berth astern of *Waverley*. *Jeanie Deans* was based at Craigendoran on the north bank of the Clyde, a throwback to the days before nationalisation when she was the pride of the L&NER. A popular Saturday excursion for her was to leave Craigendoran at 14.10, cross the river to Gourock where she picked up more passengers, thence doubling back to Dunoon, Innellan, Rothesay and round Bute clockwise (outwards via Garroch Head) to Tighnabruaich, where she arrived at 16.40. Her return left Tighnabruaich at 17.25, took her through the Kyles of Bute and back to Rothesay, following which she retraced her course back to base where she arrived at 19.55. In 1963, the fare cost 9/- (45p). She was amongst the fastest of the Clyde excursion steamers and, in her day, probably the most popular of them all.

Keith Abraham

23

30th September 1969 found *Glen Sannox* (1957) operating from Fairlie Pier as at Ardrossan, the weather was too stormy. There had been several weather-related disruptions that month. At one time, especially in the 1960s, plenty of sailings came and went from Fairlie, including some of those to Millport (Cumbrae), Brodick (Arran) and Campbeltown. In winter, Fairlie was a regularly used pier as it was more sheltered than Ardrossan where there was a risk of bad weather blowing-in overnight, thus trapping the Arran vessel.

Joe McKendrick

The new boat for Arran, *Caledonia* (ex-*Stena Baltica* and informally, *The Londoner*) at Gourock where she was officially commissioned on 28th May 1970. Almost certainly, this scene is preparatory to that event but unfortunately, the slide is not dated. She was built for the Swedish Stena A/B Gothenburg in 1966, initially for their service from Tilbury and Southend to Calais, but later she operated on their Kattegat route from Gothenburg to Frederikshavn. She was the first through-loader bought for the fleet and she could efficiently empty a full vehicle deck in 20 minutes – a speed unprecedented in the history of side loading using slow lifts and before that, stout planks of wood.

Joe McKendrick

A picturesque view taken at Brodick, Arran on 16th April 1990, with snow on the hills. *Isle of Arran* has just cleared the berth and *Waverley* is making a quick approach with a strong wind blowing from astern.

Joe McKendrick

Glen Sannox (1957) standing in for *Isle of Arran* (1984) at Ardrossan in October 1988. This was the final chance the writer took to sail in *Glen Sannox*, which was taken out of Scottish service the following year, sold to Arab owners and registered in Panama with the name *Knooz*. She met her end on the reef outside Jeddah in 2000, by which time she had had several changes of name, the last being *Al Basmalah*.

Ken Angus

On a scheduled sailing from Douglas, *Snaefell* (1948) is arriving at Ardrossan on 15th July 1977. She had just one more month before being taken out of service and scrapped by Rochdale Metal Recovery at Blyth, to where she was towed in 1978.   *Ken Angus*

Ben-My-Chree departing from the Montgomerie Pier, Ardrossan on 6th June 1976, with Capt. Bernard Quirk in command. The spiral loading ramp is full of motorcycles signifying a busy TT sailing. Peter Corrin was chief officer and can be seen right in the fo'c's'le. That year, Capt. Jack Ronan was master of *Manx Maid*. It was Steam Packet practice for second officers to take the helm for arrivals and departures to provide them with experience for when they eventually were elevated to master.   *Ken Angus*

Claymore is at Ardrossan with traffic for the Isle of Man TT races on 11th June 1995. That summer, in a combined Steam Packet/Caledonian MacBrayne joint effort, *Claymore* sailed south from Ardrossan at 08.30 on Saturdays for the eight-hour crossing to the Isle of Man. She spent the night at Douglas (with passengers in berths aboard if booked) and then returned to Ardrossan next day at 11.30. Much credit is due to David Dixon, then CEO of the Isle of Man Steam Packet Company and his Caledonian MacBrayne counterpart for planning and executing this welcome enterprise. *Joe McKendrick*

Rothesay was a popular destination for organisations in Belfast and its environs who frequently chartered Isle of Man boats for day trips from Ulster to Firth of Clyde ports. This is the Steam Packet Company's turbine steamer *Manxman* (1955) with Capt. Tom Corteen in command, running a Christian Endeavour Charter on 16th July 1969. Having spent a glorious day on beautiful Bute, some 2,000 passengers wait to embark the ship for their voyage back to Belfast. *Joe McKendrick*

On arrival from Douglas, Isle of Man, a trip of six hours duration, the Steam Packet Company's *King Orry* (Cammell Laird (Shipbuilders & Engineers) 1946) has turned outside Ardrossan harbour and is coming in astern. She lasted in service until the end of the 1975 season when she was withdrawn. Sold first to R. Taylor & Son, Bury, she went to Glasson Dock – where she spent time ashore on a mud bank as she had broken her moorings in a gale on 2nd January 1976. She was refloated and finally towed to the River Medway where she was broken up in 1979.

Joe McKendrick

The Isle of Man Steam Packet Company's steam car ferry *Manx Maid* (1962) is coming alongside at Greenock on 4th September 1970 as stormy conditions had forced her to divert from Ardrossan – a difficult port the enter (and importantly, to depart from) in bad weather.

Joe McKendrick.

Lady of Mann (1930) is seen here with whistles blowing, telling rope men and last-minute passengers that she is about to depart from her berth at the Montgomerie Pier, Ardrossan. This is 15th August 1971, her last ever departure from Ardrossan. On 17th August 1971, Capt. Tom Corteen took her away from Ardrossan. On 17th August 1971, Capt. Tom Corteen took her away from Douglas to Barrow to lay-up pending confirmation that the Company's new ship (*Mona's Queen*, 1972) would be delivered on time. She was then towed to Arnott Young's ship breaking yard at Dalmuir on the Clyde, where she arrived on the last day of December 1971. Thankfully, her bell was rescued by marine engineer John Arnold and subsequently donated to the Manx Museum. *Joe McKendrick*

This is Oban in the summer of 1971 with MacBrayne's *Claymore* just off her berth. The heaving line for her bow rope is being retrieved ready to be thrown again, to enable her to be made fast while her master looks on patiently, making sure she does not drift onto *King George V* where the photographer was standing.

Joe McKendrick

Iona (1970) arriving at Oban on 17th July 1974. As built, she had a dummy funnel on her wheelhouse but this was removed during her 1975 overhaul. She lasted in the CalMac fleet until October 1997, having served on most of their main routes somewhat unremarkably. She was sold to Pentland Ferries for service as *Pentalina B* running across the Pentland Firth to Orkney. Later she saw service at Dover and elsewhere before going to the Cape Verde Islands, where she finally stranded in 2014.

Ken Angus

Balmoral seen at Oban's North Pier on 30th April 2000.   *Joe McKendrick*

The stately *King George V* arriving at North Pier, Oban in September 1972.   *Joe McKendrick*

Lochiel (1939) at Port Ellen, Islay, on 28th September 1969. Being a Sunday, the ship remained tied-up all day. There is quite a sea running and the ship is heaving at her moorings, stern squatting down, bows rising. Had she been in service, her passengers would have had a rough trip ahead. For almost all of her career with David MacBrayne she was the mailboat serving Islay from West Loch Tarbert. Rendered redundant and replaced by the car ferry *Arran* after the end of the 1969 season, *Lochiel* was sold to new owners for service to the Isle of Man from Fleetwood. *Lawrence MacDuff*

Pioneer (1974) arriving off Armadale, Skye from Mallaig in a gale on 20th June 1979. She was built as a stern-loader but for this service she was fitted with a side-loading hoist, which was later removed. She then saw service on many Caledonian MacBrayne Firth of Clyde routes and services to the Islands before being sold to Corlett Lines, São Tomé and Príncipe in 2004, and given the new name *Brenda Corlett*, named after the owner's wife. *Lawrence MacDuff (both Ken Angus Collection)*

The North Company's (The North of Scotland, Orkney & Shetland Shipping) *St. Ola* (1951) seen at Stromness in May 1969. She was the second ship to bear the name, sailed in all weathers and was a firm favourite with islanders. She was immortalised in Alistair McRobb's lovely book *The Second St. Ola*. The North Company was taken over by Coast Lines in 1960, who themselves were subsumed into P&O Steam Navigation Company in 1971. *St. Ola* was sold for further service as a survey ship in 1975, renamed *Aqua Star*. She was eventually scrapped in Vigo, Spain in 1987.   *D.W. Greenslade*

Another of the North Company's fine ships, *St. Ninian* (1950), seen at Kirkwall in 1969. Unusual for this company, the ship was twin screw but for the *St. Clair* (p.62) which followed her, they reverted to single screw. A typical week's service for *St. Ninian* began at Leith on a Monday, then called at Aberdeen before crossing to Kirkwall, on to Lerwick and then return. Sold in 1971, she crossed the Atlantic to begin a new career in Canadian waters which lasted eight years, after which for many years, she sailed around Galapagos renamed *Buccanero*. She was reported scrapped at Guayaquil, Ecuador in 1991.   *D.W. Greenslade*

Two views of the wooden-hulled *Loch Arkaig* in dry-dock at Lamont's on 14th October 1978 for her annual overhaul.   *Ken Angus*

The date is 21st April 1981 and the magnificent *Prince Ivanhoe* (ex-*Shanklin*) is coming astern at Govan dry-docks' entrance, having completed her dry-docking, overhaul and survey in one of the three dry-docks operated by Clydedock Engineering. She was soon to set off for Bristol for the start of her new career in the 'Waverley Organisation'. It was a period of such hope and expectation that was so cruelly dashed a few months later on 3 August 1981, when she struck rocks in Port Eynon Bay, South Wales, was safely beached but in the end, had to be abandoned to the underwriters.   *Joe McKendrick*

BB Shipping's excursion ship, *Queen of Scots*, was already forty-four years old when this photograph was taken showing her in dry-dock at James Lamont & Co., Greenock, in May 1979 in readiness for her forthcoming summer season based at Dunoon. Her planned destinations that year included Kilcreggan, Helensburgh, Largs, Rothesay, Tighnabruaich and Millport. She was built as *Coronia* in 1935 for service from Scarborough. In 1968 she was sold to Crosons for service at Bournemouth, Swanage and the Isle of Wight renamed *Bournemouth Queen*. McAlpine's bought her in October 1974 for their oil rig workers on the Clyde at Ardyne. The following spring, she was renamed *Queen of Scots*. To provide limited cover for the *Waverley*, damaged by grounding on 15th July 1977, *Queen of Scots* was chartered and was in use until 31st August 1977; the next day, *Waverley* returned to service. Following the failure of BB Shipping in 1980, she has been named *Rochester Queen* and served as a restaurant ship on the Thames and more recently as Headquarters of the Medway Yacht Club where she remains.

Joe McKendrick

In one of Lamont's two dry-docks at Greenock the car ferry *Arran* received an overhaul between 6th and 22nd April 1972, in readiness for another season on the West Loch Tarbert service to Islay, Gigha and Jura.

Joe McKendrick

Loch Seaforth (1947) in dry-dock at Lamont's, Greenock, in February 1971. She was built to withstand the worst Scottish winter weather and was utterly dependable. She had two more seasons in service after this photograph was taken, by which time her design was proving old fashioned and the needs of the motor car and its driver had by then to be accommodated.   *Joe McKendrick*

Loch Seaforth (1947) laid up in Greenock's East India Harbour in April 1972. She had finished her time on the Stornoway run on 30th March 1972 and was relieved by *Clansman*, many of her crew transferring to the new *Iona*. After routine maintenance, *Loch Seaforth* proceeded to Oban at the end of May, where she was needed for the Coll and Tiree service. The following year she sank and was later scrapped at Troon.   *Joe McKendrick*

Preparing for what would prove to be her final season in commercial operation, *Duchess of Hamilton* is in one of Lamont's two dry-docks at Greenock in early February 1970. *Joe McKendrick*

This is one of Lamont's two dry-docks at Greenock with MacBrayne's turbine steamer, the stately *King George V* (1926) entering dry-dock in March 1970, the year in which she made a unique charter cruise from Ayr to Bangor, County Down, from where she sailed back across the North Channel to off Portpatrick before returning to Bangor and Ayr.   *Joe McKendrick*

MacBrayne's mailboat, *Claymore* receiving attention in one of Lamont's dry-docks, in October 1971. Latterly, they operated two adjacent dry-docks at Greenock: 370' and 360'.
Joe McKendrick

Townsend's *Dragon* (1967) on 14th June 1986.   *Lawrence Macduff (Ken Angus Collection)*

Until their closure in 1988, the dry-docks at Govan could accommodate all but the very largest vessels then afloat. There were three dry-docks measuring respectively: 560ft, 575ft and 880ft. Hopefully one day, they may be restored.

Ulster Queen (1967) leaving Clydedock Engineering's facility at Govan on 24th February 1979, having completed her annual overhaul. Her sister ship *Ulster Prince* (1967) had received attention there earlier in the same month.   *Joe McKendrick*

This is Belfast, Donegall Quay, in June 1963.
The Isle of Man Steam Packet Company's
Mona's Isle is due to sail and will depart
shortly as soon as the fairway is clear. *Duke of
Lancaster* is backing up to berth alongside
Duke of Argyll, which is lying ready with her
side doors open awaiting passengers who will
have to cross her deck. *Ulster Prince* and *Royal
Scotsman* with some coasters complete the
magnificent spectacle.   *Peter Sunderland*

Chapter 2

In and around the Irish Sea, Isle of Man, the North West and Wales

The coal-fired *Duke of Argyll* (1928) in Belfast Lough in July 1955. She had one more year in service before her successor with the same name came into service.

H.M. Rea

Duke of Rothesay (1928) at Harland & Wolff, Belfast on 21st April 1952, where she was receiving overhaul and survey.　　*H.M. Rea*

(Above) *St.Andrew* (1931) berthed outside *Duke of Lancaster* (1956) at Donegall Quay, Belfast on 19th April 1957.   *H.M. Rea*

(Below) *Duke of Lancaster* (1956) fitting out at Harland & Wolff, Belfast with HMS *Glory* being de-commissioned astern.   *H.M. Rea*

(Top) This is the same day in June 1963, as the double page spread on p.40. The photographer is aboard *Duke of Lancaster*, which is arriving from Heysham. She is going astern as she approaches Donegall Quay, Belfast, where she will come alongside *Duke of Argyll* and double-berth. Burns & Laird Lines' *Royal Scotsman* will shortly be loading for Glasgow, and lies astern.   *Peter Sunderland*

(Bottom) The venerable *Lairds Isle* (1911, ex-*Riviera* – 1932) departing from Donegall Quay, Belfast in 1955 on Burns & Laird Lines' daylight sailing to Ardrossan.   *Peter Sunderland*

A colourful parade of shipping at Belfast's Donegall Quay in the summer of 1955. From the left looking down Donegall Quay (ultimately towards the sea): *Lairdswood* and *Royal Ulsterman* for Glasgow occupy the Burns & Laird Lines' berths, next are British Railways' impressive *Duke of Rothesay* (1928) and their cargo vessel *Slieve Bearnagh* – both serving Heysham – and finally the stern of the old *Ulster Monarch*, bound for Liverpool, that night.

Peter Sunderland

Duke of York followed by *Princess Margaret* departing from Donegall Quay, Belfast in 1939, just before the start of the Second World War. Both vessels were running to Heysham, made possible by the arrival of the short-lived *Princess Victoria* (Wm Denny & Bros, Dumbarton 1939) on the short sea route from Stranraer.

H.M. Rea

St. Patrick (1948) berthed alongside the *Duke of Lancaster* at Belfast on 9th May 1959. She had arrived with a contingent of Territorial Army soldiers from Wales via Fishguard. *Irish Coast*, belonging to Coast Lines, is on the left.

H.M. Rea

Henry Rea was on the 'monkey island' of the Isle of Man boat to photograph this splendid mid-1950s Donegall Quay, Belfast panorama. Immediately beyond the Manx boat is *Ulster Monarch* (1929), then *Duke of Lancaster* (1928), *Slieve Bearnagh* (1936) and berthed farthest to the left are ships of the Burns & Laird Lines. Interestingly, upon the withdrawal of the Steam Packet ship *Tynwald* after the 1974 summer season, her triple chime steam whistle was removed before she went to the shipbreaker's and transferred to the car ferry *Ben-My-Chree* (1966), which had previously only been equipped with a somewhat hoarse-sounding steam siren.

H.M. Rea

Princess Maud (1934) going astern, towards Donegall Quay in the distance on the right. Originally she was built to partner *Princess Margaret* on the Stranraer to Larne route. After the Second World War she spent much of her time at Holyhead, running to Dun Laoghaire and latterly at Heysham on the Belfast service, where she is seen in this image. Until 1959, when the Fishguard to Waterford service ceased to carry passengers, she relieved *Great Western* too (page 84).

H.M. Rea

Two of Ferran's launches are hard at work helping the old *Ulster Monarch* turn off Donegall Quay. Before the days of ferries having bow thrusters, and with calling for tugs being expensive and frowned upon by shipowners, the best a ferry captain could hope for was a harbour launch to take a rope ashore and then giving a little extra effort by pushing. By any standards, these were big vessels for masters to handle almost unaided but they generally managed, whatever the weather.

H.M. Rea

River Lady II , seen here at Glasson Dock, was one of many small, wooden warships which became available after the Second World War. She was converted for civilian use at Brixham in time for the 1947 season and later was running trips from Ipswich and Harwich, where she was owned by Devon Star Shipping, who also had the better-known *Torbay Prince*. She then went to Holyhead and from 1963, she remained at Glasson Dock for many years, before ending her days at Lancaster where she caught fire and was demolished.

Richard Danielson Collection

Ulster Lady with a good crowd aboard, seen running an excursion to view the shipping at Donegall Quay, Belfast. She had been converted for civilian use at Portsmouth for the summer of 1948. At the time, she was named *Tay Lady*, having briefly been *Royal Tay Lady*. A year later and renamed *Ulster Lady* she went to run trips from Belfast and Bangor, Northern Ireland. After just one season she was moved to the Clyde running excursions from Greenock to Rothesay. As may be seen from the photograph, her alterations were extensive with a new superstructure adding considerably to her top hamper.

Richard Danielson Collection

The former Fairmile *Pendennis* had a nomadic existence and she is seen here at Blackpool in the summer of 1948, running a trip from the North Pier for her new owners, The Blackpool Steam Navigation Co. For 1949, 1950 and 1951, she was chartered to the Falmouth Boat Building Co. and ran popular trips for them in and around the River Fal, certificated for 134 passengers. Later she was reported to be in the ownership of Mr W.R. Metcalfe, who also owned the former British Yard minesweeper renamed *Regency Belle*.

Richard Danielson Collection

Paul Clegg captured many fine photographs during his travels as a coastal shipping journalist and photographer.

(Above) This is looking across the River Lagan to Donegall Quay, right in the heart of vibrant Belfast. *Lion* was running from Ardrossan and is seen with one of the two Belfast Steamship Company's car ferries, *Ulster Queen* or *Ulster Prince*, which were maintaining the overnight Liverpool service. The three ships were delivered new in 1967. Nowadays, the ferries are berthed much nearer the mouth of the river.

(Right) *Lion* is approaching Donegall Quay.
  Both: *W. Paul Clegg*

(Right) Preston docks on 17th April 1970, with the Atlantic Steam Navigation Company's *Ionic Ferry* running from Preston to Larne, *Barbel Bolten* on charter to them, and other coasters including Coast Lines' *Spaniel* on the far right. Still very busy when this photograph was taken, the docks officially closed in 1981 with the loss of hundreds of dock workers' jobs.

Peter Sunderland

(Below) The wharf at Fleetwood with the Isle of Man Steam Packet Company's *Mona's Queen* alongside on a day trip to the island. Beyond is the North Euston Hotel, a lovely relic of the days when the railway companies owned their own hotels and still well worth a visit to this day. With the imminent arrival of the company's first car ferry, *Manx Maid, Mona's Queen* was sold in November 1962 and renamed *Barrow Queen* for her delivery voyage to Greece. She was then renamed *Carina* for service in the Mediterranean as a car ferry; later, as *Fiesta* she became a full-time cruise ship. The Knott End ferry *Caldervale* owned by Fleetwood UDC is anchored off.

Peter Sunderland

Duke of Rothesay II (1928) and the Ferguson Bros-built hopper, *Laga II* (1955) are on Heysham's North Quay in the summer of 1956. The 'Duke' would shortly be scrapped at Milford Haven but *Laga II* had many more years ahead of her, both here and later on the South Coast. Her sister, the newer *Red Nab*, came from Appledore in 1960.   *Peter Sunderland*

Taken shortly before she was retired from service in August 1956, the coal-burning *Duke of Lancaster II* (1928) is on Heysham's South Quay. She was broken up at Briton Ferry later the same year.   *Peter Sunderland*

This splendid photograph captured by Peter Sunderland in 1962 is one of a series taken showing the handsome *Duke of Lancaster* (1956) shifting berth with the aid of the British Transport Commission's harbour tug *Ramsden* (1934). There is a gale blowing across the harbour and even though it is around low water and the ship is partly sheltered by the dock wall, her master would not want to try the manoeuvre without assistance. Unlike some other Irish Sea ports, at Heysham there were no separate berths for arrivals and departures but a spare vessel often lay at the other side of the harbour on the North Quay and had to be moved to the South Quay for service. *Duke of Lancaster* was configured somewhat differently from her two sisters in that she could be quickly converted for cruising duties when she was not required on any of the passage services. She lasted in service at Heysham until the passenger route to Belfast ended in 1975, thereafter serving Fishguard and Holyhead until November 1978. Sold on to Empirewise Limited, she was towed to Mostyn on the River Dee where she remains, having endured, now virtually abandoned, for almost forty years.

Peter Sunderland

Together at dawn for one of the last occasions at Heysham's South Quay in July 1965, *Princess Maud* is seen alongside *Duke of Argyll*. With the advent of the car ferries, 'Maud' would shortly be sold and renamed *Venus* (later *Nybo*). *Peter Sunderland*

Laying-by at the Fish Quay, Heysham on 19th July 1970, *St. David*, still wearing her old Fishguard-Rosslare livery, lacks employment and is available for sale. *Peter Sunderland*

Heysham's South Quay on 19th July 1970. The harbour works for the new ro-ro service are still in the process of being completed but amidst the building site, the proud *Duke of Lancaster* is ready to sail. *Peter Sunderland*

Having completed her final sailing from Belfast to Heysham the day before, *Duke of Rothesay* (1956) is leaving her home port of Heysham on 2nd March 1975, for the final time, destination Holyhead. She began her career as one of three sisters (the others were *Duke of Lancaster* and *Duke of Argyll*) replacing their coal-fired namesakes on the normally overnight passenger route to Belfast. Typically a speed of 14 knots was sufficient speed for the night crossing but their turbines could produce 21 knots when required. Preparatory to her taking up the Fishguard to Rosslare car ferry service, in 1967 she was sent to Cammell Laird's for conversion to a side-loading car ferry for which her main deck was gutted. Five years later she was given a stern door. She also frequently served on the Holyhead to Dun Laoghaire car ferry service. Towards the end of her career on 28th June 1974, she paid a surprise ten day visit to Dover, where a ship was urgently needed to provide the service to Calais, before returning to Holyhead on 8th July 1974. In September 1975, she went to Barrow to lay-up pending sale and was scrapped at Faslane the following month.

W. Paul Clegg

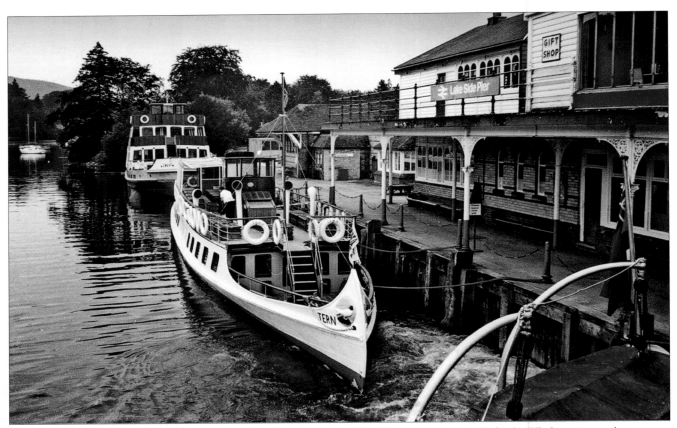

Although going back some forty years, the scene showing *Tern* at Lake Side Pier at the bottom end of Lake Windermere remains virtually unchanged to this day. *Swan* has her wheelhouse (newly added in the 1970s) and is in the livery adopted during the period when Sealink owned the steamer services as successors to British Railways and their earlier constituent railways.   *W. Paul Clegg*

Swan canting at Bowness, Windermere, on 7th April 2017, using her bow thruster to save damaging the pier structure during every manoeuvre when hauling round on their ropes, which had been the previous age-old practice.   *Richard Danielson*

A tranquil scene at Glenridding, Ullswater, on 12th April 2011. *Raven* and *Lady of the Lake* are on the far side of the pier, while the erstwhile Plymouth trip boat, *Western Belle* in the lay-by berth, receives repairs to her main engine.   *Richard Danielson*

Lady of the Lake at full speed on Ullswater on 9th April 2011, as she approaches Howtown where *Western Belle* has just called with the photographer aboard.   *Richard Danielson*

(Top) The Birkenhead Corporation ferry *Overchurch* sails for Woodside in rough weather, while the incoming ferry may be seen on the left approaching the Liverpool Landing Stage. The Wallasey County Borough Council ferry *Royal Daffodil II* is in the distance on the far side of the river. These days, the ferries would not normally attempt to sail in these conditions.   *Ray Pugh*
(Bottom) At the end of May 1997, *Balmoral* was in the North West running a successful series of trips from Liverpool (where she is seen in this photograph) and Llandudno. As a result of the Transport Act 1968, the two Mersey ferry operators had merged under the Merseyside Passenger Transport Authority and became Mersey Ferries, whose *Woodchurch* is about to berth.   *Joe McKendrick*

(Top) A foggy evening on the Mersey with *Snowdrop* (the former *Woodchurch* 1960-2003) displaying her newly adopted "dazzle paint" in the gloom on 8th January 2017.   *Richard Danielson*

(Bottom) *Royal Iris of the Mersey* (the former *Mountwood* 1960-2001) has just departed from Woodside on 18th March 2013, and will head up river past Cammell Laird's shipyards before turning to port and heading back to Liverpool Landing Stage. There is an excellent café and restaurant with river views at Seacombe ferry terminal.   *Richard Danielson*

Royal Daffodil II was built for Wallasey Borough Council by Cammell Laird's Birkenhead in 1934. Sunk by bombing on 8th May 1941, she was raised a year later and, following a lengthy refit, returned to service on 2nd June 1943. She was renamed *St. Hilary* in 1957 to free the name for the new ferry then under construction at Port Glasgow and was broken up at Ghent in 1962. *Fred Plant*

The Birkenhead Corporation ferry *Bidston* (1933), seen at Liverpool on 23rd Aug 1938 with plenty of passengers for Woodside. She was the last of five near sister-ships, the others being *Hinderton* and the rather smaller *Upton* (both 1925), *Thurstaston* and *Claughton* (both 1930). *Fred Plant*

The Isle of Man Steam Packet Company's *Lady of Mann* (1930) was a magnificent ship and is seen here in the 1960s alongside the famous floating landing stage at Liverpool, set-off perfectly against the backdrop of Liverpool's famous, and now listed, waterfront buildings. On the left with the clock and 'Liver Birds' on top is the Royal Liver Building. In the middle is the Cunard Building that once was the headquarters of the eponymously named shipping company. On the right is the domed building that was for many years the headquarters of the Mersey Docks & Harbour Board.

Ray Pugh

The Steam Packet Company's veteran *Victoria* (1907) was originally built for the South Eastern & Chatham Railway and was transferred to the Southern Railway fleet following the 1923 Grouping. The Steam Packet Company bought her in 1928 and following exemplary war service, she remained on the Isle of Man routes operating every summer until 1956, when she made her final sailing on 17th August that year. She is anchored in the River Mersey, probably awaiting the tide so that she can enter Birkenhead docks for laying up and this is where the writer, his brother Martin, who went on to become a chief engineer with Clan Line, and his father visited her in December 1956, after which she was towed to Barrow for scrapping.
Richard Danielson Collection

St. Clair (1960) is at Liverpool, Princes Dock on 21st February 1970, when she was deputising on the Belfast Steamship Company's nightly run to Belfast. *St. Clair* normally operated the Aberdeen-Shetland service. She was sold to Kuwait owners in 1977 and renamed *Al Khairat*, and was scrapped at Gadani Beach in 1987. *Lancashire Coast* lies opposite – she was carrying freight to Belfast in this era of a varied career within the Coast Lines Group.
Peter Sunderland

St. Seiriol arrives at Douglas, Isle of Man on 2nd July 1946 and lists heavily to starboard as all her passengers crowd towards the steeply sloping gangways. Capt. Dop supervises from the bridge wing.
Frank Thornley

Night scene. *St. Trillo* sharing the dry-dock with a tug and a freighter.
Frank Thornley Collection

St. Seiriol with *St. Trillo* alongside in the Morpeth Branch Dock, Birkenhead. This is 1962 and as an economy measure *St. Seiriol* would not be commissioned this season and is for sale. She would be towed away for scrapping that November.
Audrey Stephenson

The Liverpool & North Wales Steamship Company (L&NWSS)

St. Seiriol leaves the Alfred Lock, Birkenhead on 13th November 1962, towed by the Smit tug *Ebro*, bound for Ghent and the shipbreaker's yard. A small crowd has gathered to send this highly popular old ship off on her final voyage to oblivion.   *Liverpool Echo*

By now running for P.&A. Campbell, successors in North Wales to the L&NWSS, the purchase of *St. Trillo* from the liquidators saved her from following her fleetmates to the scrapyard. She is paying one of her occasional visits to Holyhead during a coastal cruise on 5th July 1967. It looks as if the photograph was taken from the mailboat berthed ahead of her. The arriving mailboat would berth on the other side of the harbour with its own railway platforms and then be moved across on her ropes to this side, ready for the next departure.

Raymond Brandreth

These two fine photographs were taken within minutes of each other on 22nd August 1980. *Ben-My-Chree* (shown in both photographs), with Capt. Jack Ronan in command, was taking the 09.00 Liverpool sailing. Capt. Peter Corrin in *Mona's Isle* tells the writer that they left the No. 4 Berth on the Victoria Pier at 08.36 with 1,170 passengers bound for Dublin. The on-pier wind was strong that morning and a high tide meant the forward belting of his ship was above the pier. Under these conditions a confident master would go astern, along the length of the pier, and using a stern rope would back round the end of the pier, exactly as is happening in this photograph, until the ship was facing to sea. Capt. Jack Ronan, with whom the writer is also in regular contact, says the Manx terminology for the manoeuvre is to 'Stroog' or in English 'to drag along'. What a morning for ship photography it turned out to be. Over on the north side of the King Edward Pier, *Manxman* (second boat to Belfast with Capt. T. Vernon Kinley) was next to carry out a similar manoeuvre to Capt. Corrin's. Before all this had happened, *Mona's Queen* (first boat to Belfast with Capt. Bernard Quirk) left the south side of the King Edward Pier at 08.10, followed by *Manx Maid* (Capt. Ken Bridson or Capt. Edward Fargher) to Ardrossan from the No. 3 Berth astern of *Mona's Isle*. She too canted round the knuckle of the Victoria Pier and then proceeded to sea bow-first. Capt. Jack Ronan then took *Ben-My-Chree* to Liverpool at 09.00, leaving just the cargo boat *Conister* in Douglas Harbour – she would sail to Liverpool at 20.00. A total of around 6,000 passengers and their vehicles departed safely in 45 minutes using five magnificent passenger vessels, three of which canted round the knuckle of their pier. Those really were the days!

Lawrence MacDuff, both Ken Angus collection.

The world famous Isle of Man TT Races calls for some highly imaginative planning of schedules. In earlier times, when the Steam Packet Company had, say, eight passenger vessels at its disposal, being able to carry 10,000 motorbikes and 30,000 passengers in two weeks was not a problem, as well as being highly lucrative. These days, with two passenger vessels (one of which is a high speed craft while the other is a combined passenger and freight vessel), they have been known to charter tonnage to cover the busiest sailings. Here we see *Stena Caledonia* (1981, ex-*St. David* 1991) on 8th June 2008, when the vessel was chartered to make a number of journeys to Douglas in connection with the TT. She did the same in 2007 and 2009.   *Richard Danielson*

(Above) *Tudor Prince*, laid up at Ramsey, Isle of Man on 15th March 1981, was built as *Torbay Prince* in 1947 for Devon Star Shipping (Mr & Mrs J. Kerr) by M.W. Blackmore & Son, Bideford and ran for them for many years in and around Harwich Haven and the River Stour. Then, still in the ownership of Kerr family, she was based in Torbay and ran in conjunction with the Western Lady fleet. In 1963, she went back to Harwich and the Harwich & Orwell Navigation Co. instead of *River Lady II* (p.49). Operating at Tenby and Milford Haven came next. Thereafter, *Tudor Prince* was owned by the Pill family on the River Fal for many years where she recently ended her days. Having been stripped of her engine, which was sold for further use, her hull was beached up river from Falmouth in the creek at Old Kea and is now in private ownership.

Richard Danielson

(Above right) Built by Philip & Son, Dartmouth as *May Queen* in 1946 for the Oreston & Turnchapel Steamboat Co., this vessel initially ran local services in Plymouth waters. Her owners were later wound up and in 1957 she was bought by the Millbrook Steamboat & Trading Co. for similar work but was renamed *Eastern Belle*. Later ownership saw her pass to Dart Pleasure Craft and Plymouth Boat Cruises, before going to G.H. Ridalls & Sons, Dartmouth, who painted her bright red and renamed her *Totnes Princess*. In 1998/99, the main fleets of Dartmouth-based pleasure boats were taken over by Dart Valley Railway PLC, rendering all but the most suitable vessels redundant.

Richard Danielson

In September 2000, Capt. Stephen Carter of the Laxey Towing Company inspected *Totnes Princess* which was then lying at Old Mill Creek, Dartmouth and she was purchased and renamed *Karina*. After 18 successful years running summer trips and excursions in Manx waters she suffered storm damage in the winter of 2017/2018 and was offered for sale. *Karina* was sold for further service in faraway West Africa and at the time of writing was waiting for a window of opportunity to begin her long relocation journey. Photograph taken on 30th July 2016.

Jennie Williamson

Ship photography often takes some intricate planning but this occasion, on 9th May 2000, was relatively easy, requiring just a pleasant day trip aboard *Balmoral* from the Isle of Man to Whitehaven, where this fascinating Greek-flagged ship, *Thraki II*, was tucked away at the back of the inner harbour. She had visited the Isle of Man the previous summer and it became known that she was constructed in Russia in 1994, where she was built to carry 260 passengers, whilst sailing at 30 knots. There was a plan for her to be renamed *Celtic Princess* and to run trips across the Irish Sea to the Isle of Man and Ireland, as well as some coastal cruises towards Scotland. She was a very lightly built craft drawing only 2.5m and sadly, it proved impossible to get agreement between the authorities, the owner and the proposed operator for getting the work done to enable her to have the necessary passenger certificates. *Richard Danielson*

This is Fred Olsen's *Bollette*, originally Sally Line's *Viking V* (1974), a beautiful ship chartered by the Isle of Man Government at a reported cost of £1 million to safeguard against a threatened NUS strike and to provide tourist accommodation during the busy 1988 TT Races that May and June. She ran a number of trips from Holyhead to the island, also from Liverpool and Belfast, carrying a very creditable 5,298 passengers and their vehicles. At the beginning of her visit the writer was aboard for a public trip north to Ramsey Bay, which showed her to be a remarkably comfortable, well appointed Norwegian ship. The writer remembers how adept the officers and crew were, arriving at the Isle of Man – a place they had never seen – and immediately running to and from the island and ports never visited before either as if it was something they did every day. Highly impressive! *Richard Danielson*

Manx Line was a brave attempt by island businessmen and major freight hauliers to bring about a cheaper, more efficient ferry service to the Isle of Man. In 1978 they purchased from Aznar Line, Bilbao, Spain an ideal ship named *Monte Castillo* (1976), which was renamed *Manx Viking*. The English base for the new service was at Heysham, with its excellent links to the UK motorways and rail system. When she was running well there was no nicer way to cross the Irish Sea and hauliers appreciated the speed with which their trailers could embark and disembark at the end of the voyage. Being a one-ship fleet, Manx Line, brought a succession of interesting ships to the island when *Manx Viking* was off service for any reason and their subsequent link up with Sealink gave them a pool of vessels to enable the service to continue without too much interruption. Here we see *Viking Victory*, chartered from Townsend Thoresen, covering the service on 16th April 1981; she came when *Earl Godwin* (below) had to leave. *Manx Viking* had just returned from Holyhead where she was given the Sealink livery for the first time.
Richard Danielson

Sealink's delightful *Earl Godwin* (1966) was another ship brought in to cover for the *Manx Viking* while she was away at Holyhead in the spring of 1981. She was here immediately before the *Viking Victory* (above). *Earl Godwin* had originally been the beautifully appointed Swedish *Svea Drott*. The writer was aboard for a public viewing on 29th March 1981 and for a round trip sailing to Heysham three days later, when this photograph was taken from the bridge wing. *Earl Godwin* arived in India for scrapping in August 2018.
Richard Danielson

Manx Viking setting sail from Douglas on 31st January 1982, bound for Falmouth, where she was to undergo overhaul and survey. Sealink's *Ailsa Princess* has been brought in to maintain the Douglas to Heysham link while *Manx Viking* is away.
Richard Danielson

This is Douglas with *Manx Viking* departing the No. 1 berth on 24th March 1984. She is passing the missionary ship *Logos*, which was visiting and later that day the writer enjoyed a very pleasant evening chatting to her master, Capt. Tage Benson and learning of the work they did around the world. She had been built in 1949 as the Danish trading vessel *Umanak*, linking Greenland with the outside world. She was a fine, strong ship but, on 5th January 1988, *Logos* ran aground in atrocious weather conditions in Tierra del Fuego, at the bottom of South America. Mercifully no lives were lost but the ship had to be abandoned.
Richard Danielson

Some would say looking her best in the Steam Packet livery but with the Manx three-legged symbol on her funnels, *Manx Viking* has just left Douglas on Easter Saturday, 1986. Later that year she was sold to Norwegian owners and renamed *Skudeness* Three years later and having been sold again and temporarily given the name *Ontairo I* she crossed the Atlantic. She was renamed *Nindawayma* for service in Owen Sound, Canada. After three years service, she was laid up and for fifteen years did little but be cannibalised for parts before eventually being dismantled and scrapped.
Richard Danielson

A fine, wonderfully nostalgic view of Holyhead Harbour and its station, almost certainly taken just before the Second World War, with London Midland & Scottish Railway excursions advertised. *Scotia* was lost at Dunkirk on 1st June 1940 and she is seen here, it is thought, in the arrivals berth with the cowls having been removed from her funnels. One of the other (active) sisters, *Cambria* or *Hibernia*, has been pulled across the harbour on her ropes and is lying in the departures berth ready to sail that night. There was a fourth sister, *Anglia*, but she was laid up at Barrow when relatively new. She remained very underused until 1935, when after ten years of virtual inactivity, she was towed from Barrow to Troon for breaking up.

J.O. Minards

St. David (1947) is coming alongside the Carlisle Pier, Dun Laoghaire arrivals berth. Since 1969, she had been providing additional capacity from Holyhead (later from Heysham after the fire which destroyed the Britannia Bridge over the Menai Strait), when she had recently been displaced at Fishguard by the converted *Duke of Rothesay*. In early 1964, *St. David* herself had been converted to a side-loading car ferry with vehicles initially using the old quayside cattle ramps. As soon as the arriving passenger ship had discharged her passengers at Dun Laoghaire, she would be worked round the end of the Carlisle Pier to the other side from where, now facing bow-out, she would depart. The harbour railway station was arranged the same way so that arriving and departing passengers' trains were close at hand. *St. David* was sold to Greek owners, part of the Chandris Group, in 1971.

W. Paul Clegg

Dublin's North Wall is the backdrop for this post-war photograph, with three ships belonging to British & Irish SP Co: The cargo vessel *Kerry* and the passenger ship *Longford* (the former 1906-built Belfast Steamship Company's *Heroic*, later *Lady Connaught*), which latterly ran the Liverpool to Dublin route in support of the new *Munster* and *Leinster*, one of which is berthed ahead of her. *Longford* was scrapped at Barrow in 1953.

H.M. Rea

This photograph shows how conveniently the railway harbour stations were positioned adjacent to the ships. This is Carlisle Pier, Dun Laoghaire on 22nd May 1971, with *Hibernia* alongside. Passengers are disembarking from *Hibernia* with some joining the trains while others leave the harbour area on foot. Later she will be worked astern round the end of the pier and having backed all the way round to the other side, will be facing seawards, ready to depart on her next voyage, as *St. Andrew* is in the photograph below.

Peter Sunderland

St. Andrew seen in the departures berth at Dun Laoghaire, probably on 12th March 1966, when she had made a special trip from Fishguard.
St. Andrew remained on her normal Fishguard to Rosslare run until the last two days of 1966, when she made what should have been her final trips and she was then laid up. However, she was able to relieve *St. David* once more in March 1967, just before her own passenger certificate expired for the last time. She was scrapped at Antwerp in June 1967.

H.M. Rea

Outside Dun Laoghaire Harbour, *Princess Maud* is just completing a daylight crossing from Holyhead on 6th August 1965, with Cunard Line's *Caronia* lying-off during a round Britain cruise. *Caronia*, affectionately given the sobriquet 'the Green Goddess', had two more years ahead of her before being sold. There followed a miserable chapter in her career culminating in her being sold for scrapping in Taiwan in 1974 but she capsized off the harbour at Apra, Guam and was broken up in-situ.

H.M. Rea

Cambria is at the arrivals berth at Holyhead in September 1963, with crew members looking on as a Ford Zephyr 4 is off-loaded by crane onto the quayside. The new car ferry service did not begin until the summer of 1965, by which time vehicle traffic on offer was such that a full hold, crane-loaded on and then off again at journey's end, could take two hours. *Cambria* made her last passenger sailing on 7th September 1975, soon after which she was laid up in Barrow awaiting disposal. Renamed *Al Taif*, she was sold to Saudi Arabian interests the following January and was later reported sunk in Suez Roads in 1981.

H.M. Rea

Cambria departing from Dun Laoghaire, her crowded decks suggesting that this may be a capacity sailing – she was licensed to carry 2,369 passengers. She is leaving astern rather than ahead which was more normal if the vessel had been warped round the end of the Carlisle Pier, bows to seaward ready for her departure.

H.M. Rea

St. David alongside in 1959, proudly flying the flag of the Fishguard & Rosslare Railways & Harbours Company at her mainmast. The F&RR&HC was an 1893 joint venture between Britain's Great Western Railway and the Irish Great Southern & Western Railway. On her bow, she carried the crest of the GWR, managers of the operation until it passed to the British Transport Commission's Railway Executive upon nationalisation in 1948. As an economy measure described by the BTC as "unification of control" the London Midland Region took over control of the Irish Sea shipping operations of the Western Region (and the Southern Region took over the Western Region's English Channel shipping operations) shortly after nationalisation. Passengers using the GWR boat train from London, Paddington and other major cities alighted alongside the ship. In those days, vehicles were crane-loaded and carried in the ships' holds. Later, *St. David* and her older running mate *St. Andrew* were able to side-load cars, but it was not long before the vehicles on offer required far greater capacity. The two vessels operated opposite each other overnight, each making a single crossing most nights, with some additional daylight sailings in high season. In winter the service left Fishguard on Monday, Wednesday, Friday nights and left Rosslare on Tuesday, Thursday and Saturday nights.
Peter Sunderland

Another splendid 1959 study, showing *Great Western* (1934) in the famous buff and black British Railways livery. She was originally owned by the GWR (not the joint F&RR&HC venture) and operated alone on the Fishguard to Waterford service, making a single crossing one day and returning the next. After nationalisation when British Railways' LMR (see above) took over her control, they had a problem as masters of their other passenger ships were paid according to the speed of their ship. The old *Great Western* was too slow for any previously known pay scale. In the photograph, she has just had the accommodation that was previously housed in her stern completely removed to facilitate the carrying of more railway containers. This meant that her crew took over her passenger spaces in the main superstructure and she would, thereafter, never carry passengers again; previously she could carry a total of 450 passengers in two classes. In the process, she lost two of her six lifeboats and she later lost another pair, leaving just two.
Peter Sunderland

Chapter 3

In and around Britain's South West, South Coast and the Channel Isles

Glen Usk (1914) was one of Campbell's most popular steamers and is seen here on 21st August 1935, with a good crowd aboard.

Fred Plant

The veteran *Ravenswood* (1891) in the old Merchants Dock, Bristol on 24th September 1955. A few days later she was towed away to Newport to be scrapped.

Fred Plant

This is Clovelly in May 1963. Campbell's magnificent paddle steamer *Bristol Queen* (1946) is hove-to off the breakwater and her passengers are coming ashore by tender. This ship, together with her near sister *Cardiff Queen* (1947), arguably represented the best of Britain's excursion steamer fleet. Large, fast and comfortable but being too expensive to operate in a climate of dwindling passenger numbers, sadly they lasted only about twenty years.

D.W. Greenslade

P.&A.Campbell's directors recognised the benefits of smaller, diesel-powered excursion ships and in a few short years, all their steamships were replaced by motorships. This, the first of their replacements, was *St. Trillo*, which was acquired from the defunct Liverpool & North Wales Steamship Company. She is seen at Barry Pontoon, during her first Campbell's season, 1963.   *Richard Danielson Collection*

Laid up together at Barry in the winter of 1970/71, Campbell's three motorships slumber peacefully. In the right-hand photograph, nearest the camera is *Balmoral* being prepared for the coming season. Ahead of her lies *Westward Ho* (formerly Red Funnel's *Vecta*), also seen in the left-hand photograph; sadly she would only last one more year in active service but she then had static roles for a further quarter century before being scrapped at Torpoint, Cornwall. Farthest from the camera is the two-funnelled *St. Trillo*. She had been inactive since the end of the 1969 season and with her Crossley machinery removed, was eventually renamed *Thrillo* and towed away to Dublin to be burnt out and then scrapped at Hammond Lane Foundry in 1975. Both:
Richard Danielson

Devonia, originally *Scillonian* (2) (p.95), was built for the Isles of Scilly Steamship Company in 1956 for their service from Penzance to St. Mary's. When her replacement, *Scillonian III*, was ready and in service in May 1977, P.&A. Campbell paid £150,000 for the older vessel and she joined the White Funnel Fleet. She ran for Campbell's (and on charter to the oil support industry) in the Bristol Channel and on the River Thames. On this sailing in August 1978, Keith Adams was aboard *Balmoral* and both ships passed at close range off Combe Martin, a few miles east of Ilfracombe. In 1982, *Devonia* was sold to Torbay Seaways who renamed her *Devoniun* and ran her successfully from Torquay, mostly to the Channel Islands before replacing her with a larger vessel, *Hebrides*.   *Keith Adams*

Balmoral in her time with P.&A.Campbell retained the open car deck aft, on which, in her Red Funnel days, she used to carry up to a dozen cars on the Southampton to Cowes service. This is Swansea on 30th April 1972, the day of the National Trust Charter to Lundy, which was a complete sell-out.   *Richard Danielson Collection*

(Left) *Tri Star* sitting on the mud in the harbour at low water in Padstow in 1980, before the lock gate was fitted (work starting in 1988). (Right) Setting off from Padstow Harbour on a busy trip down the River Camel and out to sea on 26th August 1985. In 1990, *Tri Star* was sold for further service at Ullapool, where renamed *Summer Queen* she remained for many years before moving to Whitby in 2016, where she is now operating for the friendly people at Whitby Coastal Cruises.   *Richard Danielson*

Jubilee Queen returning to Padstow after a busy trip down the Camel Estuary to sea and then along the North Cornwall coast. She was built at nearby Wadebridge in 1977 by the Chapman & Hewitt boatyard and remains a fine looking, well maintained ship, licensed to carry 200 passengers. Before she was built, Padstow trips were run in an assortment of smaller vessels including a former RNLI lifeboat which, whilst noisy, gave a very exciting voyage. The erstwhile *Queen of Cornwall* of Padstow, now named *Esk Belle III*, operates alongside her former arch rival, *Tri Star*, at Whitby (see above).   *Richard Danielson*

P.&A.Campbell organised some innovative trips using their charismatic ships on unusual sailings. What represented the first post-War sailing from Cardiff, Weston-Super-Mare, Ilfracombe and Penzance to the Isles of Scilly took place on the weekend of Friday 17th May 1963, aboard the paddle steamer *Bristol Queen* (1946). A special Class IIA certificate for 144 passengers and 41 crew was issued, matching the capacity of her six lifeboats. Here she is on her return from the Scilly Islands on the morning of Sunday, 19th May 1963. She had spent the night berthed alongside *Scillonian* (2) and her passengers were boarding for a departure at 09.30 to Ilfracombe, Barry and Clevedon, where she was timed to arrive at 21.45 that evening. Two years later, on 8th August 1965, she made a trip to the Cornish port of Padstow on charter to the PSPS with 750 passengers. The Scilly Isles trip was repeated in 1967 but towards the end of the season, major paddle wheel problems forced her early retirement. She was considered too uneconomic to repair and both she and her near sister ship, *Cardiff Queen*, were sold and eventually scrapped.   *Keith Abraham*

IOSSC Headquarters, St. Marys, Scilly. 2011.

Richard Danielson Collection

(Opposite bottom) *Queen of the Isles* (1964) is at St. Mary's, Scilly, the same pier as in the photograph of *Scillonian* (2) (opposite top), in the summer of 1966. With the green hulls are the inter-island launches *Tean*, at the pier, and *Lyonesse*, moored to the buoy. *Queen of the Isles* was built to help accommodate the anticipated growth in the population of the Scillies and the need for building material to be shipped. She also inaugurated some day trips from St. Ives and was chartered by Commodore Shipping in the Channel Isles but eventually was put on charter to P.&. Campbell operating on the South Coast, the Thames and at North Wales. In 1970 she was sold to new owners and sailed out to Tonga under her own power. She must have had her successes as a number of owners operated her in Fijian, Solomon Islands and Australian waters before she finally grounded in a hurricane and was wrecked over twenty-five years after leaving UK waters for the last time.

D.W. Greenslade

(Above) The 1956-built *Scillonian* (2) at St. Mary's, Scilly with the inter-island launch *Tean* alongside on 9th October 1973. Interestingly, the open decked *Tean* was a former Royal Navy heavy duty launch and held a Class IIA passenger certificate for 50 passengers. When deputising for *Scillonian*, *Tean* had been known to make some heroic crossings to Penzance in bad weather. When *Scillonian* was replaced by *Scillonian III* in 1977, she went on to have a long and varied career serving the Bristol Channel, the Thames and Scotland for P&A. Campbell, Torquay and the Channel Islands for Torbay Seaways, then Orkney and Shetland for Norse Atlantic. Thereafter, she was in the Adriatic, followed by West African waters and finally back in the Black Sea off Bulgaria until 2004, when she was reported to have finally sunk.

Richard Danielson Collection

This is Falmouth, one of Britain's biggest natural deep water harbours. (Top left) *St. Gerrans* (1927) with *Princessa* (1921), which was originally a ferry in Portsmouth, berthed at the Prince of Wales Pier in August 1987, ready to run local excursions. The *St. Gerrans* eventually became a private motor yacht and *Princessa* remains on the River Fal.
(Top right) *Tudor Prince* has passengers aboard returning from her Helford River trip in July 1983 (p.76).
(Above) *New Princess Maud* (1950) returns to Falmouth from St. Mawes on the other side of the harbour in the summer of 1983. She remained working on the River Fal until sold to Scottish owners at Tobermory in 2006 and was renamed *Sula Mhor*. She was sold on again to new owners, Calum's Sea Trips, Plockton, arriving there in February 2009. At the end of September 2012, whilst on a fishing trip in Loch Carron, the ship grounded on rocks and as she was making water, had to return to Plockton where her passengers safely disembarked and the vessel began to settle by the stern. The incoming tide then submerged the ship. The Kyle lifeboat had been launched but the *Sula Mhor* had been evacuated and then beached before it arrived. She was repaired and returned to service.

Richard Danielson

Nicholas Horne and his wife Faye covered all sorts of industrial and archeological photography in and around South Devon, Dartmouth and Totnes, in addition to the usual round of portraits, families and weddings. Here are scenes of the launching of two Mersey ferries at Philip & Son Dartmouth. (Top left) *Woodchurch* on 29th October 1959, for Birkenhead Corporation; her sister ship *Mountwood*, launched 6th July1959, is on the left, fitting out. (Top right and above) *Egremont* launched on 10th December 1951, for Wallasey County Borough Council. She too had a sister ship, *Leasowe*, built at Dartmouth and launched on 18th May 1951. The earlier Wallasey pair suffered from the fact that there was no walkway for seamen going forward to handle the bow ropes. They had to push their way through the often crowded forward saloon, not an easy task when the ship was full, or move perilously along outside, on the rubbing strake. This was corrected in the design of the later Birkenhead sisters. At the time of writing in autumn 2018, *Egremont* remains at Sharpness where she arrived at the end of 2016 to undergo major restoration. After leaving the Mersey ferry service, she had been moored in Salcombe Harbour since 1976 as a floating yacht and dinghy base. Unfortunately, her restoration has now stalled, and she has been refused permission to return to Salcombe.

Nicholas Horne

The Birkenhead ferry *Woodchurch* is in the floating dock at Sandquay, on the Dartmouth side of the river. She looks to be almost complete, having been launched on 29th October 1959. She was handed over to her owners on 2nd May 1960. The floating dock was originally constructed in 1885 and had been in use on the River Tyne. It became part of the Philip & Son business in 1924. They had no other dry-dock and acquiring the facility had been considered a necessity. It was dismantled and scrapped in 1961.

D.W. Greenslade

Coral Star III in the River Dart off Kingswear on 24th July 1975. She had been built as *Poole Belle* by Bolson's, the well-known boat-builders of Poole in 1948, for service in their fleet operating trips taking in Swanage, Bournemouth, Poole and the Isle of Wight. From 1958, they were operated by a newly formed company named Croson, with which Bolson's retained a strong connection. She was sold in 1964 and had several owners and names before coming to Paignton and Torquay in 1972, where she became *Coral Star III*. She went on to serve in Scotland and later at Bristol as *Avon Venturer II* for many years.

Ken Angus

This is Dartmouth Quay on 21st June 1981. *Dartmouth Castle* appears to be coming alongside with just three passengers visible on deck. She had been built in 1948 by Philip & Son, Dartmouth, whose shipyard was close by, for the River Dart Steamboat Company. Upon their ceasing to run steamer services after the 1974 season she was sold to the Millbrook Steamboat & Trading Company, Plymouth, who extensively rebuilt her superstructure, but a year later she returned to the Dart in the ownership of Dart Pleasure Craft, who were the de facto successors of the old River Dart Steamboat Company at Dartmouth. She remains on the river in the ownership of the Dartmouth Steam Railway & River Boat Company, who acquired the business of the combined Millbrook and Dart Pleasure Craft companies in early 1999.

Berthed astern of *Dartmouth Castle* is G.H. Ridalls & Son's *Queen of Helford* (1960), which later became *Tamar Belle* at Plymouth, and is now back at Falmouth where she first began serving the river she was named after. She is now in the Falmouth Pleasure Cruises Fleet (J.&F. Pill) along with the lovely old *Princessa*. To the right in the above photograph (alongside the ferry pontoon) is *Adrian Gilbert* (1957). She and her sister ship, *Humphrey Gilbert*, were built for the British Railways Kingswear to Dartmouth crossing but were sold to Dartmouth Borough Council (now part of South Hams) in 1972 when BR sold the Paignton to Kingswear railway line to Dart Valley Light Railway plc. *Adrian Gilbert* is now *Pride of Falmouth*, whilst *Humphrey Gilbert* is now named *Edgecumbe Belle* and operates the Stonehouse Quay, Plymouth to Cremyll ferry.

Ken Angus

The Higher Dart Ferry was built in 1960 and operated by Philip & Son the shipbuilders. She has left the Kingswear slipway and is headed for Dartmouth. Diesel-electric machinery was installed and she was propelled with side paddle wheels and guided on cables (not chains). These have been known to break occasionally, leaving the vessel almost impossible to control before she can be brought to a halt somewhere down river. In June 2009 she was replaced by a new ferry built in Falmouth, capable of carrying some thirty vehicles, twice that of the 1960-built ferry.

Richard Danielson

This is Dartmouth on 24th July 1975. *Pride of Paignton* was a wartime Fairmile B (ML 492) built in 1942 by Aldous Successors, Brightlingsea (some sources say Brooke Marine, Lowestoft). She was the Royal Navy's first Rescue Motor Launch. In 1946 she was sold and converted for civilian use and became *Pride of Paignton*, running morning, afternoon and evening cruises from Paignton and Torquay around Torbay, to the River Dart most afternoons, where she would go up river as far as Dittisham, and in the morning, along the coast as far as Teignmouth. The writer made several trips in her in the late 1960s and noted she was several knots faster than the similar 'Western Ladies'. She followed this sailing pattern for some thirty years but was eventually taken out of service and sold to become a private yacht named *Mars Petra*. She was at the boatyard at Bursleden, River Hamble when she sank in 1981 and was eventually scrapped.

Ken Angus

The coal-burning *Totnes Castle* (1923) is seen on the stone grid beside the River Dart Steamboat Company's depot at Hoodown, on the Kingswear side of the River Dart. She lasted in service until 1963. She then served briefly as an accommodation vessel for the Kingswear Sailing School, moored in the River Dart. That venture failed and she was sold for scrapping at Sutton Harbour, Plymouth. She was towed away by the tug *Anthony* but during the tow to the shipbreaker's, she foundered off Hope Cove in bad weather and was lost.   *D.W. Greenslade*

In this early colour transparency, the railway-owned ferry *The Mew* (1908) is approaching Kingswear towards the end of her career, sporting her new wider funnel and extra height wheelhouse. She provided the link between the GWR station at Dartmouth with the railway itself, which only reached as far as Kingswear on the opposite side of the river. She originally had saloons fore and aft and an upper deck reaching almost the full length of the ship but the saloon and upper deck at her stern were removed after the First World War and her deck was strengthened to allow her to carry a few road vehicles, including the railway's own delivery lorries. Most private cars crossed the river either on the Higher Dart Ferry run by Philip & Son or the Lower Dart Vehicle Ferries run by the local council. However, a few could be carried aboard *The Mew* and were driven aboard via the often steeply sloping pontoon bridges normally used by foot passengers. She made her last journey on 8th October 1954 and was subsequently scrapped.   *Richard Danielson Collection*

The Millbrook Steamboat Company's *Eastern Belle* was originally *May Queen*, dating from 1946. She is seen here at Phoenix Wharf, Plymouth on 26th July 1975, waiting for her next trip. The Dockyard Cruise was the mainstay of the business, although trips out beyond the breakwater to the River Yealm and up the Tamar to Calstock and Morwellan Quay were also offered. At one time only the flush-decked boats were allowed to make the voyage to the River Yealm which could be very rough but latterly, as the writer can attest, even those with an open foredeck made the excursion. From 2001 she went to the Isle of Man operating as *Karina* of the Laxey Towing Company (p.76). *Ken Angus*

The writer had been sailing on the Plymouth-based trip boats for seventeen years before locating Southdown Quay. By sea, Southdown Quay, where many of the Millbrook Steamboat Company boats would spend the night or lie off duty if the tides were right, was only just beyond Cremyll on the Cornish side of the River Tamar but by road, the journey called for a trip across the Torpoint Ferry and a circuitous drive down miles of unmarked country lanes. This photograph depicts *Southern Belle* (two masts), *Eastern Belle* and beyond them, *Queen Boadicea II* (p.141) on the evening of 2nd September 1985, moored at Southdown Quay. *Richard Danielson*

This is Phoenix Wharf, Plymouth on a busy summer Saturday, 26th July 1975, looking towards the famous Mayflower Steps on the left and on into Sutton Harbour, which nowadays is protected by a lock gate. In those days it was common to see half a dozen tour coaches drawn up on the adjacent roadway disgorging their passengers, with the same number again waiting to take their place. Nearest the camera is *Southern Belle*, vacating Phoenix Wharf to allow *Eastern Belle* to come alongside. Beyond is *Plymouth Belle* with the new yellow motif on her funnel, departing for her cruise, whilst *Devon Belle* has moved out of the way as she was berthed outside. The Millbrook Company had a quaint practise of sailing an idle ship to off-Plymouth Hoe where she would display a huge banner stating 'Dockyard and Warship Cruises' with an arrow pointing to Phoenix Wharf and repeatedly sounding the ship's whistle to attract attention. The banner can be seen furled on the upper deck rail of *Southern Belle* and on full display on *Devon Belle*.

Ken Angus

This is Torquay in August 1958, with *St. Patrick* alongside ready to run one of her special excursions. The stern of *Kiloran II* is just visible on the left, still with her lifeboat slung across her transom and this was removed shortly thereafter, leaving just a rusty streak where once the steel davits had been. The Western Region of British Railways relinquished management of its Fishguard ships to the London Midland Region (see page 84) but it was made clear that the latter were acting on behalf of the Western Region. *St. Patrick* and *St. David* remained in the ownership of the Fishguard & Rosslare Railways & Harbours Company, a British/Irish Railways joint venture. The Fishguard 'Saints' retained their red funnels (and the proud GWR shields carried on their bows) at this time, unlike the rest of the nationalised fleet which mostly carried the buff/black livery. In 1959, *St. Patrick* was bought by the British Transport Commission from the joint venture company and her funnel livery was changed to the standardised buff/black. Thereafter, *St. Patrick* was a Southern Region vessel covering most of its routes at one time or another.

D.W. Greenslade

Canberra's delivery voyage from Belfast to Southampton demonstrated that, being of a relatively new design and layout, with her machinery and funnels athwartship and well aft, and very fast at nearly 30 knots, her bow planed up and rose almost out of the water. She was considerably bigger and faster than the revolutionary engines-aft *Southern Cross* of 1955. *Canberra* proved to have 500 tons too much weight near the stern. A lot of heavy, expendable luxuries were permanently removed and then 500 tons of concrete were pumped into her bow spaces to help keep her trimmed. For the whole of her career, she was therefore too heavy so needed more depth of water, meaning that many small harbours throughout the world were never open to her. After this remedial work was done, from Southampton, she went to the Clyde for speed trials which were regarded as acceptable (if not excellent) and the ship was handed over to P&O SNC and steamed gracefully back to Southampton for the second time; on view where anyone could show an interest.

This slide was taken when the former Red Funnel paddler *Princess Elizabeth*, now based at Torquay, and over a hundred other small craft turned out to see the then brand-new *Canberra* cruise slowly through Torbay on 22nd May 1961. So, she was on her second voyage, this one from the Clyde where she had run her speed trials begun on the previous day, Whit Sunday 21st May 1961. According to Dawson in his fine P&O book, she sailed past the Isle of Man through Douglas Bay and, keeping close in where the depth of water permitted, she rounded Land's End on Whit Monday morning and sailed gently along the South Coast, slowing down to a near standstill anywhere small boats had congregated to view her. That must have been quite a spectacle.

D. W. Greenslade

Pride of the Bay was built in 1938 as *Leven* for the Caledonian Steam Packet Company and *Devon Princess* (1945) was a former wartime Harbour Defence Motor Launch (HDML), at Torquay's Haldon Pier on 29th July 1975. *Ken Angus*

Western Lady (ML535) setting off from Torquay on a well-patronised excursion on 29th July 1975. *Ken Angus*

Kiloran II (1941) departing from Torquay on an evening cruise early in her Devon career, was another Fairmile B (ML253). She was converted for civilian use first as the yacht *Lepanto*, later for the 1956 season as the trip boat *Cambrian Prince* based mainly in North Wales. She came to Torquay for Devon Cruising Company in 1957 (still registered in Liverpool) and in 1963 she was sold to Cornish Sea Cruising, having been succeeded by *Bateau Morgat*. In June 1996 the writer made several trips on the then heavily rebuilt *Kiloran* out of Sliema, Malta, where she enjoyed another long career after leaving Cornish waters in the late 1960s.

D.W. Greenslade

Our Queen operated by J. Bolus returns to Torquay in July 1975, with a capacity load of 80 passengers aboard. She survived until 2001 when she was reported to have been broken up.

Ken Angus

Another HDML (ML1396), *Pride of the Dart* (1944), seen at Torquay on 7th August 1978, was converted for civilian use and owned by the Torbay Cruising of Paignton, whose other ship was the much larger *Regency Belle*. *Pride of the Dart* then became part of the Western Lady fleet until 1986, when J. Bolus took the vessel first on charter; later he purchased her. She was not a fast vessel but was a comfortable seaboat. On 28th June 2002, while making a trip from Torquay to the Dart (something she had done for many years), she struck the reef between the Mew Stone Rock and the shore. Taking in water, her passengers (twenty-six plus one small baby) had to be taken off by *Dart Explorer* and the Castle Ferry, which both came to her aid. With the help of the harbour authority's boat, she was then safely beached at Lighthouse Cove on the Kingswear side of the Dart.

Ken Angus

Running for Torbay Seaways the former *Scillonian* (2) was renamed *Devoniun* and based at Torquay for three seasons, 1982, 1983 and 1984, running excursions mainly to the Channel Islands. She was a tough little vessel with a long, tall fo'c's'le for added buoyancy, having been built for voyages twenty miles into the Atlantic to the Scilly Isles. Nevertheless, when it was rough, the journey to the Channel Islands, crossing a beam sea rolling in straight from the Western Approaches and piled up as the land masses of France and England constricted the Channel, made many journeys very much a trial of endurance. She was replaced by the much larger, stabilised *Hebrides* from Caledonian MacBrayne's Western Isles routes.   *D.W. Greenslade*

The stylish, erstwhile Newhaven to Dieppe joint service steam ship *Lisieux* (1952), later also operating a purely French service to Jersey and St. Malo from Weymouth, is seen at Torquay running trips on charter to French Lines (CGT) in 1965. She was sold in 1966 to Nomikos of Greece who renamed her *Apollon*. A decade later, in 1977, she was sold again, this time to Agapitos but she continued to operate the same Piraeus to Mikonos route. She remained operational until 1980 but her powerful steam turbines were hugely expensive to run and she was scrapped at Eleusis in 1982.

D.W. Greenslade

This is Haldon Pier, Torquay, in May 1967. For many years, Torquay harbour had been a popular departure point for underemployed cross-Channel boats and some smaller seagoing excursion ships. The former railway-owned Newhaven-Dieppe fast mailboat *Brighton* (1950) was by then running for Jersey Lines and, bearing the name *La Duchesse De Bretagne*. She operated between Torquay, Weymouth, Southampton and Plymouth and the Channel Isles, and across to France but had no stabilisers and could roll unrelentingly in a beam sea.   *D.W. Greenslade*

Clansman at Torquay on 1st December 1984, in the ownership of Torbay Seaways. Looking at her location in the harbour, she appears to be lowering her stern door using the dog-leg at the far end of the Haldon Pier for more steady moorings put out each side. In the event, Torquay did not want the complications of becoming a commercial cross-Channel port and the ship was sold on to Maltese owners. *Ontic* was their freighter at the time too.

D.W. Greenslade

For 1985, Torbay Seaways operated a hydrofoil named *Star Capricorn* from Torquay, which was not a great success. For 1986 the company acquired one of *Clansman's* sisters, *Hebrides*, and with the blessing of Torquay Council and the DoT she became their *Devoniun*. In 1991 she was laid up for a major overhaul at George Prior's and in 1993 was sold and renamed *Illyria* for Mediterranean service. She was eventually scrapped in Turkey in 2003. This is Torquay and the photograph is dated 24th November 1985.

D.W. Greenslade

The railway-owned *St. Julien* captured on film in beautiful, late afternoon sunlight at Torquay in the late 1950s. The dog-leg at the end of the pier is clearly shown in this image. When a vessel was surplus at Weymouth, Torquay was a favoured harbour from which to run day trips to the Channel Islands and the French coast.

D.W. Greenslade

(Above) The British Railways tender *Sir John Hawkins* (1929) was based at Millbay Docks, Plymouth. Her duties tendering ocean liners did not vary much but the tenders occasionally ran coastal excursions too. She was scrapped at Ghent in 1962.

D.W. Greenslade

(Below) On a visit to Guernsey in August 1987, the writer and his wife chose to sail from Weymouth aboard the former Ardrossan boat *Lion* (1967). By then she had been sold to Cypriot owners who had rebuilt her and renamed her *Baroness M*, then chartered her to British Channel Island Ferries who ran her under the name *Portelet* for two seasons. She was scrapped in Bangladesh in 2004.

Richard Danielson

Isle of Guernsey, one of three near sister ships built for the Southampton to Channel Isles run but also serving on the Newhaven to Dieppe route, photographed at Jersey in 1957. Of the three, this ship survived the latest in British Railways service and having finished at Jersey in May 1961, she was laid up at Southampton and scrapped at Ghent that November. In service, they were all renowned for rolling heavily and the last of the three, *Isle of Sark*, was given stabilisers to good effect, early in her career. The third member of the trio, *Isle of Jersey*, remained in service until she was sold in March 1960 and renamed *Libda*. She was scrapped in 1963 having finally taken the name *Libya*.
N.T. Parsons

Normannia in Jersey, having been temporarily transferred from the British flag to SNCF to keep the pooling and sharing arrangements in balance. She ran trips for them to St. Malo and Guernsey on 28th April 1973, before shortly returning to Sealink. She was rather unloved for the rest of her career and in the end, sailed herself to oblivion at the hands of shipbreakers at Gijon, Spain, but not before she ran out of fuel and had to meet up with a road tanker dispatched by Sealink, London to enable her to finish the journey.

Richard Danielson Collection

Caesarea (1960) and her sister *Sarnia* (1960) were the final traditional passenger ships built for the railway operated Channel Islands service. Powered by steam turbines, they represented the ultimate in design of this class of ship, once so common around our shores. The travelling public's needs had changed dramatically in the last few decades, mostly dictated by the fact that they wanted to be able to travel with their cars which these ships were not equipped to do, save for a few crane-loaded vehicles carried in their holds. The roll-on car ferry service to Jersey was inaugurated by *Falaise* in June 1973, and Guernsey followed the following late summer, soon after the start of which *Falaise* failed and was sent to Holyhead for inspection and possible repair. In the event she was deemed not to be worth repairing and went for scrap in Bilbao at the end of 1974. *Caesarea's* final sailings to the Channel Islands were at the end of the 1975 season, after which she was moved to Dover, later to be sold to Hong Kong owners. *Sarnia* was sold in 1978.

Richard Danielson Collection

The two-funnelled *Queen* with *Bournemouth Queen* beyond making for Bournemouth Pier on 27th August 1935. Both vessels belonged to Red Funnel Steamers.
Fred Plant

Cosens were owners of *Emperor of India*, which is seen arriving at Bournemouth Pier on 27th August 1937. She had been built for Red Funnel as *Princess Royal* in 1906 but had proved unsatisfactory and was returned to her builders. She was modified and lengthened to improve her speed but remained slow and was sold to Cosens & Company, entering their service in 1908.
Fred Plant

The two-funnelled *Monarch* was the first in Cosens' fleet to bear the name. Cosens were renowned for operating a fleet of delightful but elderly paddlers and *Monarch*, photographed here on 26th July 1939, was no exception. She was built in 1888 by R.&H. Green, Blackwall, London, near to what is now Canary Wharf. Despite her small proportions of 210ft by 22ft and with a gross tonnage of just 309, until the First World War she regularly made excursion trips across the English Channel to French ports, Cherbourg taking over five hours from Bournemouth Pier. To help keep her dry at sea, her fo'c's'le was enlarged early in her career and became a vantage point where passengers would congregate for great views. She had two extra lifeboats fitted in 1912, whilst the small wheelhouse seen here was added in time for the 1930 season. After 1918, she ran mostly from Bournemouth and Swanage and lasted until the end of the 1949 season, being towed to Milford Haven for scrapping the following year. *Fred Plant*

Cosens' *Consul* was another fine example of an elderly paddler doing solid service year in, year out. In this photograph she is coming astern (not a popular manoeuvre with paddle steamer captains) down the harbour at Weymouth on 23rd September 1955. Dating from 1896 when she was built as *Duke of Devonshire*, Cosens acquired her in 1938 and having renamed her *Consul* ran her mostly from Weymouth. In 1963 she was sold to South Coast & Continental Steamers and in 1965 she was sold again to become a floating accommodation vessel for Sail a Boat Holidays, when she reverted to her original name. This venture was not successful and she was scrapped at the end of 1968 by Ferry Services & Supplies, Southampton. *Fred Plant*

On this page, two very different ferries, both built about the same time by J. Samuel White's famous shipyard at Cowes, Isle of Wight.

The Poole cross harbour ferry No. 1, which had no other name and is seen here at the Shell Bay side, was steam powered and built in 1926. No. 1 lasted in service from 1926 to 1958. There have only ever been four ferries on the route and the present ship dating from 1994 is named *Bramble Bush Bay*; it can carry forty-eight vehicles compared with eighteen carried by No. 1. To this day a return voyage taking a few minutes on the ferry, saves a twenty-five mile drive. *Richard Danielson Collection*

The Southern Railway's delightful paddle steamer *Freshwater*, with the suffix *II* after her name for the last few months of service ready for the new ship to take the name, was built in 1927 and is just off Lymington Harbour station, from where she ran to Yarmouth, Isle of Wight. She lasted here until September 1959, followed by two further years, first bearing the name *Sussex Queen* and sailing along the Sussex Coast, then *Swanage Queen* serving Bournemouth, Poole and Swanage. She was scrapped at Bruges in 1962. *Keith Abraham*

This beautiful photograph shows the paddle steamers *Consul* and *Princess Elizabeth* at Weymouth in the summer of 1964. With the numbers of passengers making trips on excursion ships falling year by year, it seemed an odd move to have these two old paddlers both based at Weymouth competing for what little business there might be. On the positive side for her business, *Consul* was able to land her passengers on the beach at Lulworth Cove using the old wheeled landing boards. *Princess Elizabeth* was unable to do this but was still being marketed as 'sailing to Lulworth Cove'. The writer has an image from the late Bert Moody's collection showing her at the entrance to Lulworth Cove with paddles being kicked astern to take the forward motion off she travelled too far into the Cove and while she could retreat in a straight line astern.

Keith Abraham

Red Funnel's charismatic paddler *Princess Elizabeth* (1927) has remained the writer's all-time favourite steamer since he made a very rough trip in her to Cowes on 27th July 1954, at the age of just seven years. His report of that event marked the start of the writer's love affair with this ship and small passenger ships in general and one which has lasted him a lifetime. Here, at dusk one night in November 1967, the writer photographed the ship from the Floating Bridge at Woolston, where it was feared she would be scrapped. In the event she was sold on several times and has lasted longer in static preservation than she was active, remaining afloat and still doing business moored in Dunkirk Harbour.

Richard Danielson

Princess Elizabeth working her way round the corner of the Victoria Pier, Cowes on 13th July 1936, ready to depart, bows seawards. The Fountain Pier at Cowes and the berth across the river at East Cowes were normally the preserve of Red Funnel's ships on the passage service to Southampton whilst this, the Victoria Pier, was traditionally used by the excursion steamers. The pier survived until its demolition in 1962 but it had been in a rather dilapidated state since the Second World War, when it was taken over by the Royal Navy and visits by steamers were a rarity thereafter. Note that *Princess Elizabeth* has not yet gained a wheelhouse nor full width saloon aft.

Fred Plant

(Left) This is *Medina* (1931), which was the first motorship owned by Red Funnel Steamers. She is lying at Fountain Pier, Cowes, Isle of Wight on 22nd April 1957 and is remembered as much for her propensity to roll mercilesslay as for her slowness on passage, which could often take over an hour. She was re-engined in 1953, after which she was able to keep to the timetable fairly well.
Richard Danielson Collection

(Below) The paddle ferry *Hampton* arriving at Southampton's Town Quay from Hythe on the other side of Southampton Water on 18th July 1936.
Fred Plant

This fascinating photograph (last used in Red Funnel publicity material over fifty years ago) is of the Royal Pier, Southampton from where Red Funnel Steamers ran their service to Cowes, Isle of Wight and many excursions and docks cruises. On the left is Red Funnel's *Medina* and on the right, is Cosens' paddle steamer *Monarch*. By then Cosens had become a subsidiary of Red Funnel. In the background is the Union Castle liner *Pretoria Castle*, with the Red Funnel tug *Paladin* in attendance alongside.

The date is mid-June 1953 and the occasion is the Coronation Naval Review at Spithead, when hundreds of ships from the Royal Navy, Commonwealth and Foreign Navies, and from our Merchant Navy were gathered for Her Majesty's Review. The actual Review took place and began at 15.30 on Monday, 15th June 1953, with Her Majesty having boarded HMS *Surprise* (which was acting as the Royal Yacht) the evening before for the start of the proceedings.

Many excursion ships were doing great business for several days in the run up to the actual Review, offering trips to view the assembling fleet. On the big day, *Monarch* was running trips to see the Review from Southsea whilst *Medina* became part of the official Review fleet, anchored in the company of the hundreds of assembled Naval warships, ships of the Merchant Navy and many other paddle steamers, ferries and trip boats.

The former tank landing craft *Norris Castle* was left to plod on alone (at her effective maximum speed of 8 knots) on the Southampton-Cowes service route, as all the other ships of Red Funnel Steamers were involved in the Review in one capacity or another. The British Railways ferry *Lymington* was probably the sole ship operating on her namesake route to Yarmouth. The British Railways ferries *Brading* and *Southsea* from Portsmouth carried on running the ferry to Ryde until the latest possible moment, after which they were needed in an official capacity to carry Admiralty staff among the fleet, lined-up behind the royal cavalcade as it made its stately way up and down the lines of the assembled ships.

Pretoria Castle, together with *Orcades* and *Strathnaver*, took their places in the fleet and were carrying government officials for the day. *Pretoria Castle* alone required two trains from London's Waterloo station to convey all her dignitaries. After fireworks rounded-off the celebrations that evening, some of the ships remained in the anchorage, whilst others began taking their passengers ashore and others took the opportunity to pick up more passengers for later evening trips to see the remains of the spectacle. Life began to return to normal on the Tuesday when the whole fleet gradually dispersed. Richard Clammer, in his fine book *Cosens of Weymouth 1918 to 1996* (Twelveheads Press, 2001) tells us *Monarch* returned to Poole as she needed to take on coal for her bunkers before resuming her normal services.

Red Funnel Archives

(Opposite page) The top image shows *Vecta* on the Southampton - Cowes passage service carrying passengers, their cars (stowed forward on her partly enclosed vehicle deck) and the Royal Mail. Originally she was fitted with Voith Schneider units but was converted to diesel-electric transmission after the Second World War. The bottom image shows *Balmoral* on an excursion, bathed in glorious afternoon sunshine arriving at Shanklin Pier, in the summer of 1968. In contrast to *Vecta*, *Balmoral's* vehicle deck was aft on the main deck where she could carry about ten to twelve cars.

Both Keith Abraham

The British Railways *Sandown* arrives at Portsmouth with very few passengers aboard. *Ryde* is moored ahead on the 'hulk' outside the harbour station and ferry berth. Both ships are still wearing the time-honoured buff/black livery.

Richard Danielson Collection

Ryde and her elder sister *Sandown* were coal-fired throughout their lives. Here, *Ryde* is coming alongside Ryde Pier with a good crowd of holiday-makers ready to disembark.

Keith Abraham

Whippingham (1930) seen on 1st August 1934, ran the Portsmouth to Ryde service at busy summer weekends and excursions from Southsea. There was something wonderfully majestic about *Whippingham* and the writer saw her at Newhaven receiving attention at the Marine Workshops beneath the sheerlegs on several occasions on visits to the harbour in the 1950s. She was withdrawn after the 1962 season and broken up the next year. Her sister ship, *Southsea*, was mined on 16th February 1941 and subsequently lost.

Fred Plant

Merstone (1928) was another railway-owned ferry on the Portsmouth to Ryde service which, until 20th September 1941, she operated opposite her sister *Portsdown*. At 04.00 that morning, whilst on the early morning mail run to the island, *Portsdown* struck a mine and suffered devastating damage, resulting in the loss of the ship, her master, crew and twelve passengers. *Merstone* carried on serving the island throughout the Second World War and until after the 1948 season came to a close. She retired to the Outer Dock at Southampton where she was for sale – but found no buyers. Four years later she was towed away and scrapped. This photograph was taken on 28th August 1935.

Fred Plant

Shanklin (1924) was another stalwart on the Portsmouth to Ryde service, seen here on 18th July 1936. She was on service to the island throughout the Second World War and until the end of the 1950 season, when she was withdrawn. Cosens bought her, renamed her *Monarch* and enjoyed another decade of summer work from this coal burner. Swanage and Bournemouth were popular at the time and she and *Embassy* were kept busy there and on trips to the Isle of Wight. Overall, passenger numbers were falling away and *Monarch's* time was over. At Weymouth, she was boarded up and was ready to be towed away for scrap at the end of January 1961. In the event it was another month later that the weather moderated enough for the tow to Cork, where she arrived on 2nd March 1961.

Fred Plant

This is Newhaven where the writer was privileged to start his banking career in 1963 with the Midland Bank. The sheerlegs on the left were in use by British Railways Marine Workshops until they were cut down on 13th August 1965. This photograph, by the writer's father, shows *Arromanches* departing for Dieppe, *Brighton* (6) laying-by and the cargo vessel *Brest*, which before the days of the car ferries often carried cars in parallel with the passenger steamer, whose passengers would have to wait some hours to be reunited with the cars in Dieppe.

George Danielson

Ryde and other British Railways Southern Region ships regularly laid up in Newhaven Harbour when not required. This is the winter of 1967/68. *Ryde* was taken out of service after the 1969 season and was sold for use as a floating nightclub at Binfield Marina in the Isle of Wight. To this day, she lies there forlornly rusting away. Her older sister, *Sandown*, had survived until the close of the 1965 season and the following February she was towed away for scrapping in Antwerp.

Richard Danielson

The handsome *Brighton* (1933) and fifth to bear the name, is entering Newhaven on 30th August 1937. Sadly she was lost in a bombing raid on Dieppe on 24th May 1940.

Fred Plant

There was still hope that the former Portsmouth - Ryde ferry *Southsea* would see some sort of further service under Jim Sherwood's Sea Containers aegis when this photograph was taken at Newhaven on 27th September 1998. Various attempts to save the ship came to nought and she was eventually towed away from Southampton to Denmark for scrapping in March 2005. *Richard Danielson*

Ryde prepares for her penultimate season and is being worked on at the Marine Workshops, Newhaven, on 20th April 1968.
Richard Danielson Collection

Hengist is at the car ferry ramp, Newhaven, with *Falaise* tucked in astern. On 7th June 1972, the brand new *Hengist* was on her way from her shipbuilders, the Naval Dockyard at Brest, and called in to test the linkspan for the benefit of her sister-to-be, *Senlac*, not yet built but destined for the Newhaven - Dieppe Joint Service operated by SNCF and British Railways.

Richard Danielson Collection

Falaise is leaving Newhaven on 2nd July 1967. She had been built in 1947 for the Southern Railway routes from Southampton to St. Malo and the Channel Islands, and with comfortable cabins and lounges, she could operate day and night services. She was a popular cruise ship for British Railways off-season, visiting many interesting ports until 1963, when she was earmarked for conversion to a car ferry for the new Newhaven-Dieppe car ferry service. She had a reputation of being a difficult ship to handle going astern, and regular collisions with quay walls earned her the nickname 'The Big F'.

Richard Danielson Collection

Richard Danielson Collection

Still in her old livery with the traditional black hull and black-topped buff funnel, *Brighton* (1950) slips gently out of Newhaven Harbour in the summer of 1963. As soon as she clears the outer harbour and the once-beautiful West Beach, her master will ring down on the engine room telegraph for full speed ahead. Capable of delivering 18,500 shp, her turbines could propel her along at over 24 knots, burning fuel oil at a prodigious rate in the process. The arrival of the car ferry revolution on the route rendered her almost redundant save for running No-Passport day trips and special excursions. Her sale to Jersey Lines was announced at the end of 1966 and renamed *La Duchesse De Bretagne*, she was adapted to carry twenty-plus cars loaded over ramps near her stern and carried on deck, aft. Jersey Lines' timetable was intricate and exciting and took in Plymouth, Torquay, Weymouth, Southampton, the Channel Islands, St. Malo and Cherbourg. To make money with her uneconomic turbines, she had to carry full loads all the time – but sadly, she never did. After two seasons and with mounting debts, Jersey Lines ceased trading and *Brighton* was scrapped in 1970.

Caledonian Princess (1961) at Dover on 21st September 1981. She had been built for the Stranraer to Larne service. A victim of her own success she went on to see service on many of the British Railways shipping services to Ireland, the Channel Isles and the near Continent. Withdrawn in October 1981, she was eventually sold and in 1983, towed to Newcastle (later Glasgow, reverting to her old name) as an entertainment and leisure centre renamed *Tuxedo Princess*. In 2008 she was sold to Greek interests and was scrapped at Aliaga in 2008. *Andrew Jones*

Maid of Orleans (1949) departs from Boulogne on passage for Folkestone on 11th July 1971. She spent much of her career on this run but also served at Dover. She moved to Weymouth in June 1974 to cover for the disabled *Sarnia* on the Channel Islands service and her place at Folkestone was taken by *Duke of Rothesay*, sent down from Holyhead in another unlikely long distance ships' replacement move. Her sailing career ended on 27th September 1975 and three days later she was moved to Newhaven to lay up. On 6th November 1975, the deep sea tug *Ibaizable Tres* towed her out of Newhaven with the Sealink tug *Meeching* taking the stern rope until she was clear of the harbour and she arrived at Santander for scrapping on 9th November 1975. *Andrew Jones*

(Above left) *Canterbury* (1929) leaving Folkestone in the summer of 1958. Originally, she was Dover's Golden Arrow ship, carrying First Class passengers only. Soon after the war, her place was taken by *Invicta* and *Canterbury* moved to the Folkestone to Boulogne route, which she sailed until she was withdrawn in September 1964. The following year, still in her old British Railways livery, she was towed to Antwerp for scrapping. If a copy can be located, Henry Maxwell's fine but rare book *The Canterbury Remembered* is highly recommended. (Above right) From left to right, *Lord Warden*, *Koningin Fabiola* and *Maid of Kent* together in the Eastern Docks, Dover in August 1966. At the time this photograph was taken, the Belgian Marine Administration sailed the Dover to Ostend route relatively unmolested but later, in Sea Containers' ownership, Sealink tried to increase its share significantly.   *Both Peter Sunderland*

The Southern Railway's *Invicta* was built just before the Second World War began but did not see civilian service until after the hostilities ended. She had been built to replace the ageing *Canterbury* on the Golden Arrow service, which she finally did in 1946. Originally she burnt coal from the nearby Kent coalfields but she was converted to oil fuel after the war when she was finally given stabilisers too. She remained on the Golden Arrow run throughout her career and for a long time was the largest ship in the Southern fleet. Her final commercial sailing was on 8th August 1972 and two days later she retired to Newhaven to lay up pending sale. She was broken up in Holland, where she arrived for scrapping at the end of September 1972.   *Andrew Jones*

Another action filled photograph – this one of Calais showing the Sealink vessel *Horsa* arriving from Folkestone in early summer 1981. *Vortigern* is due to depart for Folkestone shortly. They were both working a complicated web of sailings starting their day in Ostend, thence to Folkestone, Boulogne, Folkestone, Calais, Folkestone before ending the day at Ostend. Some period railway freight wagons are on the quayside along with the moveable ramp for cars joining or leaving the French railway system.

Peter Sunderland

This is Boulogne in July 1977. *Caesarea* is just arriving from Folkestone. At the time she was running from Calais to Folkestone in the mornings, then fitting in a round trip to Boulogne before heading back to Calais. Beyond her is *Lion*, recently finished at Ardrossan and now running from Dover to Boulogne for the Normandy Ferries division of P&O.

Peter Sunderland

Richard Danielson

The last rays of sun bathe *Horsa* going astern from Boulogne on 8th December 1986, destination Folkestone. By then the schedules had been rationalised and *Horsa* was operating opposite her sister, *Hengist*, covering the Folkestone to Boulogne route with *Vortigern* providing relief when necessary. The writer and his wife had sailed out of Dover for the day aboard *Free Enterprise IV*.

Normally a Folkestone-based vessel, this is *Isle of Thanet* in Southampton Water, after turning to enter the River Itchen and now passing the entrance to the Empress Dock, just prior to entering the Outer Dock where the railway-owned ships berthed. The picture shows her with passengers probably inbound from Guernsey – the shadows/sun suggest it is late afternoon. History shows there have been a number of occasions when railway-owned ships have been moved, often hundreds of miles, in order to make a few trips on a route that had capacity problems. *Isle of Thanet* was used in this way between 1952 and 1957 sailing light from Folkestone to make just one round trip between Southampton and Guernsey per week on summer Friday nights, before returning back up-Channel. Thanks to Don Jones who witnessed the events first hand and whose encyclopaedic knowledge of Solent shipping matters is second to none.   *Keith Abraham*

The British Rail car ferry *Maid of Kent* (1959) arriving at her berth in Boulogne's Gare Maritime, Quai des Paquebots, in July 1966; seen from the foredeck of *St. Patrick* shortly to depart for Folkestone. At about this time, the photographer took photographs of *Maid of Kent* entering Dover for use in *British Nationalised Shipping 1947-1968* and its softback derivative, both co-authored with John S. Styring.

W. Paul Clegg

This is the Gare Maritime Boulogne, with *Lord Warden* (1952) alongside, wearing the traditional buff/black British Railways livery and with the fireman's helmet recently fitted to her funnel to help disperse sooty emissions. She was the first drive on - drive off car ferry built for the British Transport Commission and was the ferry in which the writer and his family first crossed the English Channel together in 1959 in a gale.
*Richard Danielson
Collection*

(Below) *Lord Warden* in the modified Sealink livery, seen powering away from Boulogne on 7th June 1969.
Andrew Jones

Kingswear Castle was usually scheduled to meet *Waverley* at least once every year while she was on the River Medway. This is one such occasion when masters of both ships skillfully manoeuvred their vessels in various spectacular but planned, safe moves giving passengers on both ships a great show. The writer, in a trip on *Kingswear Castle* in 2003 (see below), exposed four rolls of colour slide film each costing £10. Multiply that by say, 300 passengers taking photographs and you begin to get an idea of the huge economic activity generated by these fine old ships. Yet, sometimes, the many authorities involved seem to make things unnecessarily difficult for operators of historically important ships.

Joe McKendrick

This is Strood Pier, on the north-west bank of the River Medway, with *Kingswear Castle* (1924) boarding passengers for her trip down river where she would meet with *Waverley* on 5th October 2003. She was bought by the Paddle Steamer Preservation Society in 1967 from her owners, the River Dart Steamboat Company. Her steam engine was from her namesake predecessor, dating from 1904. Volunteers, supporters and corporate sponsors succeeded in almost totally rebuilding the ship, after which she ran very successfully on the River Medway from 1985. Her master and prime mover was Capt. John Megoran and he presided over finally returning her to her spiritual home on the River Dart in December 2012.

Richard Danielson

This favourite image has been chosen to close the South Coast chapter of the book as it evokes the writer's fondest memories of Southampton, the liners, Red Funnel Steamers, the Royal Pier, *Princess Elizabeth* and all the little pleasure boats that congregated just off the Mayflower Park, waiting for business in the 1950s and '60s. The Cunard liner *Mauretania* is inbound from New York preparing to berth in the New (Western) Docks where the writer and his father were invited aboard to see over the great liner and meet the captain for tea in his day room. In her berth on the Royal Pier is Red Funnel's paddler, *Princess Elizabeth* laying-by or preparing to run a Docks Cruise or excursion. If she were making a passage service run to Cowes, which she often did, she would almost certainly have been berthed at the adjacent floating pontoon so that vehicles (of which she could carry ten) could board her foredeck. Moored just off the Royal Pier are the trip boats *Shamrock* nearer the camera (in 1972 renamed *Southampton Star*) and the former Portsmouth Harbour ferry *Vesta*, which became *Kingston Belle* when at Hastings Steamers on the Thames (and since renamed *Southampton Belle*). The writer made the first of many trips in *Princess Elizabeth* and the other ships in the Red Funnel fleet in July 1954 when he was seven years old and proudly wrote a report of one such very rough trip which remains in the family archives. Visits to go aboard the liners at Southampton and elsewhere were possible on account of the writer's father being heavily involved in the training of the nation's Marine Radio Officers; the shipping companies using Marconi equipment welcomed the writer and his father at every opportunity.

Richard Danielson Collection

Queen of the South (1931, formerly the Caledonian Steam Packet Co's *Jeanie Deans* until 1965), takes on bunker oil whilst at her mooring in the Upper Pool above Tower Bridge, on 30th July 1966. Her route usually took her from Tower Pier to Herne Bay and Southend, initially to Clacton too. Despite goodwill and plenty of money invested, she only managed one further short season when, with mounting unpaid debts, was sold by order of the Admiralty Marshal and towed to Antwerp for breaking up in December 1967. Just ahead, *Queen of the Channel* is boarding passengers at Tower Pier and will soon be setting off down river once Tower Bridge has been opened for her (see p.140). *Queen of the Channel* and her two larger General Steam Navigation (GSN) fleetmates, *Royal Sovereign* and *Royal Daffodil*, operated numerous day excursions from London, Gravesend and Clacton to Southend, Margate, Calais and Boulogne, and some coastal cruises too. With falling passenger numbers and unwanted competition, the services came to an abrupt halt after the 1966 season, when all three ships were withdrawn and sold. *Richard Danielson Collection*

Chapter 4

In and around the River Thames,
England's East Coast and
Cruising BR style
much further afield

(Above) The British Railways Tilbury - Gravesend vehicular ferry *Mimie* (1927) at Tilbury in August 1963. The vehicular ferry services operated by this ship and her near sister, *Tessa* (1924), ran until the end of 1964, by which time the new Dartford Tunnel made them redundant. They were scrapped in Bruges in 1965.

(Right) The Tilbury-Gravesend ferry was also home to three elderly passenger ferries, which were displaced by three new diesel Voith Schneider ferries: *Edith* seen here, along with *Rose* and *Catherine*, all built by Whites Shipyard (Southampton) in 1961. Sea Containers and then Stena Line were successors to BR and in 1991 the ferry was sold to White Horse Ferries. *Both: Peter Sunderland*

Tessa (built in 1924 by Lytham Shipbuilding and Engineering Lytham) is departing from Gravesend in August 1963 and the approaching *Mimie* (built in 1927 by Ferguson Bros, Port Glasgow) waits to come alongside having left Tilbury on the north side of the Thames, five minutes earlier. For four years, these coal-fired veterans ran alongside the three new diesel passenger ferries until the Dartford Tunnel was completed. The vehicle ferries could carry passengers (*Mimie*: 300, *Tessa*: 250) as well as about twenty road vehicles depending on their size. Both had coal fired reciprocating machinery and could manage 9 knots, The Tilbury - Gravesend service was the writer's first local ferry having been born at nearby Erith on the south side of the River Thames and lived for the first sixteen years of his life in south-east London.

Peter Sunderland

139

The GSN excursion ship *Royal Daffodil* in her final season, seen at Gravesend for a day excursion down river and on to France in August 1966.
Peter Sunderland

The GSN motorship *Queen of the Channel* on her way down river, passes through the majestic raised bascules of London's famous Tower Bridge on 30th July 1966. This would prove to be the last season these trips were operated by GSN.
Richard Danielson Collection

(Above) The diminutive former British Railways Dartmouth ferry *Humphrey Gilbert* was earmarked along with her sister, *Adrian Gilbert*, to take over the British Railways Tilbury - Gravesend ferry. With this in mind, they were expensively given new engines and steel wheelhouses at Weymouth in 1977. The 'Humphrey' was boarded up and brought round to the Thames where she was resoundingly pronounced 'unfit' by the authorities and the plan was abandoned. Only a state-owned business could make mistakes like this and survive!

(Left) The Embankment with Thames trip boats doing good business judging by the crowd aboard *Queen Boadicea II* (p.102).

Photos:
Richard Danielson Collection

Sealink's *Amsterdam* (1950) at Parkeston Quay, Harwich in July 1967. The service to Hook of Holland was run overnight by the British ships, opposite the ships of the Dutch Zeeland Steamship Company which provided daylight sailings.   *Peter Sunderland*

British Railways Eastern Region's *Arnhem* (1947), near sister of *Amsterdam*, at Harwich in 1963. *Arnhem* remained in service until she was scrapped at Inverkeithing in August 1968. *Amsterdam* lasted a little longer but once *St. George* was established on the route with the newer *Avalon,* she was sold to a Chandris Lines subsidiary in 1969 and served as their *Fiorita*. Later she became a hotel ship in Turkey, in which role it was reported that she had sunk in 1987.   *Peter Sunderland*

Goodbye *Avalon* London, Hello *Valon* Panama – arguably once one of the most handsome ships in the British Railways fleet. Completed in 1963 for the foot-passenger era that was fast ending, she filled in her spare time with popular off-season cruising. She was converted to a car ferry in 1975 based at Fishguard (and later Holyhead). In September 1980, she was moved from Holyhead to Barrow where this photograph was taken in December 1980 and then on to Gadani Beach where she arrived for scrapping in January 1981.   *Peter Sunderland*

The train ferries ran from Harwich Town (not Parkeston Quay) to Zeebrugge and Dunkirk. This is *Essex Ferry* at the train ferry terminal in August 1963. She had near sisters, the similar looking *Norfolk Ferry* and *Suffolk Ferry*, and the more modern *Cambridge Ferry* and *Speedlink Vanguard*. After the shipping operations of Britain's railways were packaged into Sealink and later sold to Sea Containers, the train ferries were initially chartered back to British Rail but the service ended in 1987.   *Peter Sunderland*

Excursions on the Norfolk Broads have a long and interesting past, employing many different vessels. *Golden Galleon* (above – Fairmile ML162) was operated by John Knight and was based at Great Yarmouth with Southern Coastcraft's *Eastern Princess* (ML347), spending many years on the East Coast before her sale to Greek owners. *Queen of the Broads* (opposite page) and *Resolute* (below) seen at Great Yarmouth on 5th September 1957, were operated by Pleasure Steamers Ltd, running trips on the Broads and to Lowestoft and Gorleston. Another fine vessel, *Norwich Belle*, ran trips to nearby Scroby Island until 1981 and after lay-up in Tilbury, was eventually sold for further service in Israeli waters. *Fred Plant*

The future of the elderly coal-fired Humber paddle ferries had been the subject of much debate by British Railways for a while but they became victims of a coal miners strike in early 1972, as there was no bunker coal until imports temporarily eased the situation. In the event, *Tattershall Castle* was sold out of service in July 1972. She spent the last half of 1974 at Immingham, where she is seen here being refitted prior to being towed to the River Thames firstly as a floating gallery, later in the hospitality business, where she remains to this day. The writer can confirm that a meal or drinks aboard is a very pleasant experience.   *Peter Sunderland*

Lincoln Castle at Hull Corporation Pier on 30th June 1974 for a PSPS charter trip. Her damaged fo'c's'le was as the result of a collision with *Polarisman* on 23rd May 1974.   *Ken Angus*

Lincoln Castle, wearing the Associated Humber Lines' livery (but without the AHL on her funnel) has a few vehicles on her car deck aft. Taken in 1961, *Lincoln Castle* has just left Hull Corporation Pier and is navigating the sandbanks and maritime obstructions of the river, heading for New Holland on the south side. Associated Humber Lines was originally a management committee set up in 1935 by the L&NER and the LM&SR companies, together with Ellerman's Wilson Line to manage the affairs of their and their subsidiary companies' North Sea services, which would otherwise, acting independently, suffer unnecessary internal competition with each other. AHL was incorporated in 1957 to carry on doing the same job as before. The Humber ferries were managed by AHL between 1959 until 1971, when the company ceased operations and Sealink took over control. The three elderly ferries were withdrawn one by one and after the departure of the 'Tattershall', *Wingfield Castle* was next to go in 1974, her place being taken by the redundant Isle of Wight ferry *Farringford*. *Lincoln Castle* lasted until 1978 and has since been scrapped, whilst the other two survive in static preservation. *Farringford* continued a one-ship service until the new Humber Road bridge was opened in 1981 and three years later she was scrapped on the Humber, never having actually operated for Western Ferries who by then had purchased her for possible use on their Firth of Clyde ferry route.

Peter Sunderland

The old *Melrose Abbey* (1929) at Hull in 1957. She and her fleetmate *Bury* (1910) had run the tidal service from Hull to Rotterdam since time immemorial. In 1958 she was given the suffix *II* to her name and was advertised for sale when a new motorship bearing the same name was delivered. The following year, renamed *Kriti*, the old ship was sold to Typaldos Bros Steamship Company, Piraeus, and commenced a new career cruising the Mediterranean at the age of thirty. Typaldos ceased to trade in 1966 and the old *Kriti* was left to disintegrate but was eventually scrapped many years later. *Peter Sunderland*

(Above) On 5th October 1958, *Aire* (1931) inbound from Antwerp bound for Goole, was in collision with *Helene B Schupp* causing a major gash along her starboard side. Her master managed to beach her at Saltmarshe near Goole but despite all efforts she slid back into the River stern first. She was eventually partly raised and, deemed to be a constructive total loss, she was scrapped.

Peter Sunderland

(Opposite bottom) By May 1967 when this photograph was taken at Humber Graving Dock & Engineering Company, Immingham, *St. Patrick* had already led a nomadic life. Built twenty years earlier for the Fishguard & Rosslare Company, she mainly ran from Weymouth to the Channel Isles each summer. In 1959 she was 'bought' by the British Transport Commission from the F&R subsidiary and thereafter was managed by the Southern Region. In 1964 she was called upon to close the Southampton route to Le Havre and at the end of the season, closed the St. Malo services permanently too, before moving up Channel to serve Dover and Folkestone. In February 1967 she was sent to Immingham for further alterations to improve her passenger capacity on the SR routes she served. In September 1971 she was retired to Newhaven and was sold six months later in March 1972, then resold to Agapitos Bros, Piraeus and renamed *Agapitos I* for Mediterranean service. She was eventually scrapped at Perama in 1980. Berthed next to *St. Patrick* is British Railways cargo vessel *Wakefield*, being overhauled and modified for her new service between Hull and Antwerp, starting in 1968. *Peter Sunderland*

When Britain's railway companies owned and operated ships as the means of linking railheads separated by water, they utilised surplus capacity in the off-peak seasons by running many cruises to interesting, distant destinations. This is *Duke of Lancaster* during one of her 1960 Scottish Isles and Lochs cruises. She also sailed twice to Scandinavian ports that year. The ship's own lifeboats were used at anchor ports to carry passengers to and from the shore.

Richard Danielson Collection

All three of *Duke of Lancaster* Continental cruises for 1961 took in Amsterdam, where the ship is seen in this photograph and on each occasion she remained alongside there for three nights, commencing on 1st June, 7th June and 15th June respectively. The first cruise departed from Heysham on 23rd May 1961 but returned to Harwich on 4th June, from where the second and third cruises both started. The third Continental cruise that year returned her passengers to Heysham on 26th June, sailing direct from Bergen, via the Pentland Firth.

Richard Danielson Collection

Cruising BR style after 1948 was mostly carried out by three railway-owned ferries: *Falaise*, *Duke of Lancaster* and *Avalon*, although others were used at quiet times for odd excursions and day trips. This is *Avalon*, well inside the Arctic Circle, anchored in Skarsfjord in May 1971 on her way north to Narvik in northern Norway. This thirteen night cruise from Harwich called at Bergen, Narvik, Trondheim and Stavanger, before returning home. The cruise would have cost between £80 and £230 depending on the cabin grade. The same year in September, she sailed from Harwich to Lisbon, Tangiers, Vigo, St. Nazaire and back.

Richard Danielson Collection

This is *Avalon* during her 'Avalon 1973 Follows the Sun, Casbah 13-night Cruise'. She departed Harwich on 8th September and by the morning of 10th September, when this photograph was taken, she had reached La Rochelle on the Atlantic coast of France. The writer is indebted to Pascal Courtheoux, Sylvian Martin and S. Grunenwald, who are the port management at La Rochelle, for speedily identifying this berth as Mole d'Escale West at La Rochelle. The tall, grey port grain silo is by *Avalon's* bridge wing and La Rochelle is one of France's most important grain exporting ports. The rest of the cruise took in Cadiz, Agadir and Oporto (Leixoes) before returning to Harwich. The cost of this cruise ranged between £90 and £270 depending on the grade of cabin. *Richard Danielson Collection*

This is the River Tyne at Newcastle on 7th May 1983. *Waverley*, passing the moored *Caledonian Princess* (p.128), by then recently acquired by Michael Quadrini, is on her way down river and on to the Farne Islands. After completing her sailings in the North East, *Waverley* sailed north through the Pentland Firth to Fort William – a journey accomplished in near-perfect weather. A few years later, Mr Quadrini contacted the writer requesting plans of the recently redundant Isle of Man Steam Packet Company's *Manx Maid*. It had been hoped she might secure a future in static preservation in that welcome enterprise but, sadly, it was not to be and *Manx Maid* was eventually scrapped at Garston in 1986.

Joe McKendrick

Chapter 5

A few words of appreciation about some of our ship photographers who, sadly, are no longer with us

KENNETH (Ken) ANGUS

Ken Angus and I were correspondents for over thirty-five years but never met and during that time exchanged hundreds of slides not only with each other but with a wider band of like-minded photographers. At the start of the relationship it quickly became clear that there was much synergy between our respective photography interests, and whilst Ken also studied and photographed aircraft and warships in great numbers (which I did not) both of us took hundreds of pictures of excursion ships, West Country trip boats, and the Clyde 'steamers'.

Ken Angus's slides were noted not only for their excellence but for their meticulous labelling and it was a constant source of amazement to those lucky enough to be recipients of them that his painstakingly accurate labels, hand-written in tiny, quasi 6-point capital letters could be read as if typeset by a printer. Ken Angus had been a world-class senior development engineer in the aerospace industry by profession. Sadly, Ken passed away suddenly in 2015 but left a splendid legacy of maritime, naval and aeronautical photography second to none.

RAYMOND BRANDRETH

Often in the company of his mother in her lifetime and the other regular sailing contractors, Raymond Brandreth travelled the length and breadth of the country sailing in and photographing coastal passenger ships. His photographs were always fascinating and sometimes of slightly unusual subjects. He passed away some fifteen years ago.

W.P. (Paul) CLEGG

I knew Paul Clegg for many years and with the help of the late Mike Walker, hold a large collection of black and white and colour photographic negatives of short-sea shipping of all descriptions taken by him from the 1960s onwards. Paul was a great authority on coastal shipping, a trusted writer of books and articles for shipping magazines on his subject and editor of other important well-known shipping journals, including the much-missed *Ships Illustrated*. He was also an early and key member of the Coastal Cruising Association for many years.

In his time he had also been a teacher, ship broker and later a freelance journalist travelling the world. Latterly Paul lived in South Devon and was a Town Councillor in Ashburton. With his sad passing in 2010 and his encyclopaedic knowledge of his subject, the world of short-sea shipping lost one of its most dedicated and knowledgeable experts.

D.W. (Dennis) GREENSLADE

Dennis Greenslade was a prolific and talented photographer living in Devon. A skilled dental mechanic by profession, he spent six years in the RAF and later became a ship model-maker of considerable renown. Several large batches of his colour slides came on the market a few years ago. I was fortunate to be able to secure two good collections of these, covering mainly unusual shipping subjects in and around South Devon, including those taken in Torquay and Dartmouth harbours from the mid-1950s onwards and some Scottish scenes too. Dennis Greenslade was a well-respected wildlife photographer too. Sadly, he passed away several years ago.

NICHOLAS and FAY HORNE

Nicholas Horne and his wife Fay ran their well-known professional photographic business based in the Narrows, High Street, Totnes and also the camera shop in Fore Street, Totnes. Nick Horne, who was also a town councillor at Totnes, did his apprenticeship with Kodak before joining the RAF in the Second World War. Between them the firm covered all the post-war shipyard activity at Philip & Son, Dartmouth and they were both keen general, portrait and archaeological photographers too. Fay Horne was the first woman member of the British Institute of Professional Photographers. When they retired in 1984, the business was sold and I was able to purchase the whole of the shipyard-related collection of negatives, many of which later appeared in Derek Blackhurst's excellent book *Philip & Son, Dartmouth, Shipbuilders and Engineers*.

Sadly Mr and Mrs Horne passed away within a year of each other in 1998 and 1999.

In Millennium year 2000, I donated the entire Horne collection comprising several thousand shipping negatives to Dartmouth Museum, where it was all scanned by their now late and much-missed member, Gordon Thomas, and remains freely available for interested people to research and view.

JOSEPH (Joe) McKENDRICK

Joe Mckendrick and I were good friends and correspondents for over thirty-five years and during that time we exchanged many hundreds of colour slides of 'steamers' of mutual interest.

A much respected and loved teacher of chemistry and principal of pastoral care and guidance at Jordanhill College, Glasgow, Joe McKendrick shared his time and talents between the school, its students (who called him 'Dr Joe') and everything to do with 'steamers'. His great passion was for the paddle steamers *Waverley* (of which he was a director), *Kingswear Castle* (of which he was a trustee) and Britain's most widely-travelled excursion ship, *Balmoral*. He was also instrumental in the saving and restoration of Blairmore Pier. Joe took his camera with him wherever he went. Most of his collection is devoted to the Clyde steamers and *Waverley* especially, when she and her then running mate *Balmoral* began visiting ports and harbours all round the British Isles. He also photographed local and Continental school trips and educational cruises aboard *Nevasa* and *Uganda*, Scottish architecture and holidays in the Swiss Alps, where there are paddle steamers in abundance.

In his collection, most of which is now held by the Clyde River Steamer Club (CRSC), there are many fine images taken by Joe himself over some forty years and the wider collection is supplemented by many earlier specimens taken by excellent photographers, including the Rev'd Roderik Pettigrew, whom he knew well and who entrusted their collections to him. I took much pleasure in digitising, restoring and conserving thousands of these fine photographs and slides for the benefit of the CRSC. The last time Joe and I met was in April 2012. During one of our regular telephone conversations, I happened to mention to Joe that I was coming north of the border for a week in their capital. Joe immediately suggested a meeting to visit *Waverley* and *Balmoral*, in dry-dock together for the first time ever. From his encyclopaedic knowledge, Joe gave me the time of the trains from Edinburgh to Glasgow, the required change of stations (Queen Street/Central) and on towards Greenock where he said to alight at Cartsdyke and he would be waiting in his car for the short journey down to the dry-dock. In fact, Joe was on the platform when the train pulled in and, complete with hard hats, a very pleasant few hours was spent in and around the Garvel and the James Watt Dock (where *Finlaggan* lay). A late lunch was enjoyed together and Joe then drove me back to Cartsdyke for the train back to Glasgow and onwards to Edinburgh.

This kindness was so typical of Joe. Sadly, he passed away after a short illness later in 2012 but we are fortunate to have so many good things by which to remember him and his wonderful sense of humour. A great crowd of us gathered at Clydebank on Tuesday 21st August 2012, to send him on his final voyage across the Bar.

J.O. MINARDS

Mr J.O. Minards was President of the Warrington Photographic Society in 1949/50 and was an early pioneer of colour photography, as well as taking superb black and white glass plates. I bought a small collection of Mr Minards' original transport photographic work from a dealer in The Lanes, Brighton, including shots taken in Holyhead, Dun Laoghaire and Douglas, Isle of Man.

FRED A. PLANT

Fred Plant was a long-standing member of the Clyde River Steamer Club, of which he was President in the 1955-56 session. He was known for being a perfectionist with regard to his photography, discarding any pictures that he felt fell below his own high standards. He was an accountant by profession, having first qualified in law at the University of Glasgow. He took maritime and railway photographs from the 1930s onwards and in addition to all his Scottish photography, he regularly visited the Bristol Channel, South of England and Switzerland too.

Thanks to the good offices of Mr Iain Quinn, I hold a large collection of mainly medium format black and white shipping negatives taken by Fred Plant from the 1930s onwards in many locations 'south of the border'. His sad passing in April 1987 was recorded in the CRSC *Clyde Steamers Magazine* No. 24.

RAY PUGH

Born in 1908, Ray Pugh was a knowledgeable ship historian, expert maritime photographer, an enthusiastic artist and writer, and an amateur radio expert. Ray too, was a regular tripper (known as 'contractors') on the Steam Packet boats and Liverpool & North Wales steamers and when I could get away from work, I made many a trip with them all. Ray Pugh and I were in regular contact writing and on the telephone and over time, many fine photographs, slides and a range of historic marine ephemera were exchanged. Raymond's sister Barbara and nephew Gordon Ditchfield were very busy on all the steamers also and were long-time friends of the Mersey ferries, a capacity in which Gordon still does magnificent work to this day. A good gathering of us were at Birkdale Methodist Church on 19th December 2000 to pay our final respects to Ray Pugh, a venerable old gentleman.

H.M. (Henry) REA

Henry Rea was a highly-regarded teacher by profession and latterly was Head of Languages at Bangor (NI) Grammar School. He was a keen sportsman and rugby referee at school and in rugby union too, and was renowned for his fine sense of humour. For much of his life his spare time was taken up with ship and railway photography in which he was an expert and he had a number of advantageous venues (probably known only to him) where he positioned himself to secure his most spectacular shots. Renowned for his Irish Sea shipping photography, Henry Rea also visited the Continent regularly and took many photographs in and around the Channel ports.

Through the efforts of the late Mike Walker, I hold a large collection of mainly medium format black and white negatives taken over a period of fifty years by Henry Rea. Acquired separately is a collection of some of his colour slides, which came on the market several years ago. Henry Rea retired in 1977 and having enjoyed an all too short retirement, sadly he passed away in 1980. His fine photographic legacy will live on in perpetuity.

LESLIE STEPHENSON

Leslie Stephenson ran the publishing business, T. Stephenson & Son, Prescot, Lancashire. Frank Thornley was the author of the best known works on the L&NWSS, which were published by T. Stephenson & Son, along with many of the other standard works by other authors on coastal shipping subjects, including *Faithfully Yours, Manxman*, containing this writer's appreciation of the last of the classic Manx steamships. Frank Thornley was a great collector, statistician and album builder as well as a writer and when he passed away, all his albums went to Mr and Mrs Stephenson and following Leslie's sad passing, Audrey handed all the material over to me.

FRANK THORNLEY,

Author Frank Thornley, and Leslie Stephenson and his wife Audrey, were connected by many things including a long-term friendship and regular and frequent sea travel aboard the ships of the Liverpool & North Wales Steamship Company (L&NWSS) and the Isle of Man Steam Packet Company. I knew them all in this connection too and enjoyed many journeys with them and other 'regular trippers' and contractors forty years ago.

THANKS and ACKNOWLEDGEMENTS

I wish to thank retired Isle of Man Steam Packet Company masters Capt. Jack Ronan and Capt. Peter Corrin, who remain in regular contact with me. Their detailed knowledge and records of events covering many decades have been made freely available to me and are without equal. I am privileged to have known them both for over forty happy years, during which time Britain's cross-Channel, coastal and excursion ship business has changed beyond recognition.

My grateful thanks are due to both Christine Pettigrew (Joe McKendrick's cousin and wife of the late Rev'd Roderik Pettigrew, who was himself a talented steamer photographer) whom I met at Clydebank on 21st August 2012, and Waverley director Deryk Docherty (Joe's executor). They have been keen to ensure that this work becomes a reality, showcasing the specific part of Joe's collection which I gathered over the years and which they helped me to consolidate a few years ago.

Beth Angus and Debbie Mountford, Ken Angus's immediate family, ensured that Ken's superb photographic legacy lives-on and I am most grateful to them for entrusting it to my care.

Lawrence Macduff, a well-known and expert ship and transport photographer, is a good family friend of the Angus's and through that connection, many of Lawrence's fine colour slides now reside within Ken's collection under my stewardship. Thank you Lawrence for your willingness to help me in these pictorial endeavours.

Dougie and Elspeth Rea, H.M. Rea's family, have enthusiastically followed the progress of this work and I am grateful for their help, gladly given.

COVER CAPTIONS

Front: The main photograph shows *Lady of Mann* arriving at Douglas, Isle of Man on 27th October 1996, nearing the end of a very stormy crossing from Fleetwood.   *Richard Danielson*

Back: The main photograph (from an old Dufay slide) shows the majestic *Whippingham* approaching Ryde in 1937.
               Sidney Perrier, Tom Lee Collection
The other cover photographs appear in the book.

The magnificent *St. Tudno*, belonging to the Liverpool & North Wales Steamship Company, is seen approaching Llandudno on 16th September 1962. This was the last day of operations for the company, which was later wound up. *St. Tudno* never sailed again after that day and was sold for scrapping at Ghent, Belgium in 1963. Happily, her remaining fleetmate, the small motorship *St. Trillo*, was sold for further service with P.&A. Campbell Ltd (see page 91).
Cyril Perrier, Tom Lee Collection

High Water at Heysham in September 1963. The stately *Duke of Argyll* (1956) is loading for the night crossing to Belfast. The three 'Dukes' were good for 21 knots and needed this for daylight sailings but overnight 14 to 15 knots usually sufficed. The service was timed to leave Heysham at 23.55 and arrived at Belfast, Donegall Quay at 07.00.   *R.D. Charnock, Peter Sunderland collection*

INDEX

Adrian Gilbert 99, 141
Agapitos 1 149
Ailsa Princess 79
Aire 149
Al Basmala 25
Al Khairat 62
Al Taif 83
Alumchine 87
Amsterdam 142
Anglia 80
Anthony 101
Antrim Princess 78
Apollon 108
Aqua Star 33
Arnhem 142
Arran 18, 20, 21, 32, 35
Arromanches 124
Ashton 14, 15
Autocarrier 132
Avalon 142, 143, 151
Avon Venturer II 98
Balmoral 7, 21, 31, 58, 74, 77, 91, 92,
......120, 121, 155, 91, 92,120, 121, 155
Barbel Bolton 51
Baroness M 111
Bateau Morgat 107
Ben-My-Chree (1927) 65
Ben-My-Chree (1966) 26, 47, 63, 70, 72
Bidston 60
Bolette 77
Bournemouth Queen 114
Brading 121
Bramble Bush Bay 116
Brenda Corlett 32
Brest 124
Brighton (1933) 124
Brighton (1950) 109, 124, 127
Bristol Queen (1938) 14
Bristol Queen (1946) 90, 94
Bucanero 33
Bury 148
Bute 18, 19
Caesarea 113, 130
Caldervale 51
Caledonia (1934) 4
Caledonia (1966) 24
Caledonian Princess 128, 152/153
Cambria 80, 83
Cambrian Prince 107
Cambridge Ferry 143
Canberra 105
Canterbury 129
Cardiff Queen 90, 94
Carina 51
Caronia 83
Castle ferry Dartmouth 107
Catherine 138
Celtic Princess 77
Clansman 13, 110
Claughton 60
Claymore (1955) 30, 38
Claymore (1978) 2, 3, 27
Cleddau King 86, 87

Cleddau Queen 86, 87
Clutha 11 87
Columba 5, 13
Conister 70
Consul 115, 117
Coral Star III 98
Coronia/Bournemouth Queen 35
Countess Fiona 14
Countess of Breadalbane 14, 15
Countess of Kempock 14
Cowal 18, 19
Dart Explorer 107
Dartmouth Castle 99
Devon Belle 103
Devon Princess 106
Devonia 92
Devoniun 92, 108,110
Dragon 39
Duchess of Hamilton 10, 11, 37
Duke of Argyll (1956) 2, 40/41, 43, 44,
...................54, 55, 157
Duke of Argyll (1928) 42
Duke of Devonshire 115
Duke of Lancaster (1928) 52
Duke of Lancaster (1956) .40/41, 43, 44, 46,
.........47, 53, 54, 55, 150, 151
Duke of Rothesay (1928) 42, 45, 52
Duke of Rothesay (1956) 55, 81, 128
Duke of York 46
Earl Godwin 78
Eastern Belle 76, 102, 103
Eastern Princess 145
Ebro 69
Edgcumbe Belle 99
Edith 138
Egremont 97
Embassy 123
Emperor of India 114
Esk Belle III 93
Essex Ferry 143
Falaise 113, 126, 151
Farringford 147
Fiesta 51
Fiorita 142
Free Enterprise 1V 131
Freshwater/Freshwater II 116
Glen Sannox 18, 24, 25
Glen Usk 90
Glengarriff 85
Glory (H.M.S.) 43
Golden Galleon 145
Great Western 84
Hampton 119
Hebrides 13, 92, 108, 110
Helene B Schupp 149
Hengist 126, 131
Heroic 81
Hibernia 80, 82
Higher Dart Ferry 100
Hinderton 60
Hispaniola 12
Horsa 130, 131
Hotspur II 22

Humphrey Gilbert 99, 141
Ibaizable Tres 128
Illyria 110
Innisfallen 85
Invicta 129
Iona 30, 36
Ionic Ferry 51
Irish Coast 46
Isle of Arran 25
Isle of Guernsey 112
Isle of Jersey 112
Isle of Sark 112
Isle of Thannet 132
Jeanie Deans 23, 136/137
Jubilee Queen 93
Karina 74, 76, 102
Kenilworth 22
Kerry 81
Kiloran II 104, 107
King George V ....22, 30, 31, 38.
King Orry 28, 66
Kingston Belle 135
Kingswear Castle 134, 155
Knooz 25
Koningin Fabiola 129
Kriti 148
La Duchess de Bretagne 109, 127
Lady Connaught 81
Lady Magdalen 87
Lady of Mann (1930) 29, 61, 71
Lady of the Lake 57
Laga 11 52
Lairds Isle 44
Lairdswood 45
Lancashire Coast 62
Leasowe 62, 97
Leinster 81
Lepanto 107
Leven 14, 106
Lincoln Castle 146, 147
Lion 50, 111, 130
Lisieux 108
Loch Arkaig 5, 34
Loch Seaforth 36
Lochfyne 4, 8/9
Lochiel 18, 32
Lochnevis 4
Logos 79
Longford 81
Lord Warden ....129, 133.
Lymington 121
Lyonesse 94, 95
Maid of Argyll 16
Maid of Ashton 12, 16
Maid of Cumbrae 16
Maid of Kent 129, 132
Maid of Orleans 128
Maid of Skelmorlie 16, 17
Mannin 73
Manx Maid 26, 28, 51, 70, 72, 152
Manx Viking 78, 79
Manxman 27, 70, 72
Marchioness of Lorne 14

Mars Petra .100
Mauretania .135
May Queen 76, 102
Medina 119, 121
Meeching 128
Melrose Abbey 148
Menna . . . . .87.
Merstone 123
Mimie 138, 139
Mona's Isle 40/41, 70
Mona's Queen (1972) 29, 70, 73
Mona's Queen (1947) 51
Monarch (1888) 115
Monarch (1924) 121, 123
Monte Callisto 78
Mountwood 59, 73, 97
Munster 81
Nevasa 155
New Princess Maud 96
New Roseland 22
Nidawayma .79
Norfolk Ferry 143
Normannia .112
Norris Castle 121
Norwich Belle 145
Nybo 54
Ocean Coast 85
Ontario I 79
Ontic 110
Orcades 121
Our Queen 107
Overchurch 58, 73
Paladin 121
Pendennis 49
Pentalina B .30
Pioneer 32
Plymouth Belle 103
Poole Belle .98
Poole Ferry No. 1 116
Portelet 111
Portsdown .123
Poseidonia .85
Pretoria Castle 121
Pride of Falmouth 99
Pride of Paignton 100
Pride of the Bay 106
Pride of the Dart 107
Prince Ivanhoe . . . . .34.
Princess Elizabeth 105, 117, 118, 135
Princess Margaret 46, 48
Princess Maud 48, 54, 83
Princess Royal 114
Princessa (1921) 96, 99
Queen 114
Queen Alexander 9
Queen Boadicea II 102, 141
Queen Elizabeth 2 . . . . .73, 89
Queen Mary /Queen Mary II 10, 13
Queen of Cornwall 93
Queen of Helford 99
Queen of Scots 35
Queen of the Broads 144, 145
Queen of the Channel 136/137, 140

Queen of the Isles 94, 95
Queen of the South 136/137
Ramsden 53
Raven 57
Ravenswood 90
Red Nab 52
Regency Belle 49, 107
Resolute 145
River Lady II 49, 76
Riviera 44
Rose 138
Rochester Queen 35
Royal Daffodil 135/136, 140
Royal Daffodil II (1934) 60, 136
Royal Daffodil II (1958) 58
Royal Iris 73
Royal Iris of the Mersey 59
Royal Jubilee 22
Royal Scotsman 40/41, 44
Royal Sovereign 135/136
Royal Tay Lady 49
Royal Ulsterman 45
Ryde 122, 124, 125
Saint Colum 1 63
Saint Columba 8
Saint Patrick 63
Salisbury 72
Sandown 122, 124
Sarnia 113
Saturn 22
Scillonian 7, 92, 94, 95, 108, 160
Scillonian III 7, 92, 95
Scotia 80
Senlac 126
Shamrock .135
Shanklin (1924) . . . . .123.
Shanklin (1951) 10, 34
Sir John Hawkins 111
Skudenes 79
Slieve Bearnagh 45, 47
Snaefell 26
Snowdrop 59
Sound of Sleat 22
Southampton Belle 135
Southampton Star/Vesta 135
Southern Belle 102, 103
Southern Cross . . . . .105.
Southsea (1930) 123
Southsea (1948) 121, 125
Spaniel 51
Speedlink Vanguard 143
St. Andrew 43, 82, 84, 85
St. Clair 33, 62
St. David (1947) 54, 81, 82, 84, 104
St. David (1981) 75
St. Gerrans .96
St. Hilary 60
St. Julien .110
St. Ninian 33
St. Ola 33
St. Patrick 46, 104, 132, 148, 149
St. Seiriol 65, 66, 67, 68, 69
St. Trillo 65, 66, 68, 69, 91

St. Tudno 64, 65, 66, 156
Star Capricorn 110
Stena Baltica 24
Stena Caledonia 75
Strathnaver 121
Suffolk Ferry 143
Suilven 12
Sula Mhor 96
Summer Queen 93
Surprise (H.M.S.) 121
Sussex Queen 116
Svea Drott .78
Swan 56
Swanage Queen 116
Talisman 14
Tamar Belle 99
Tattershall Castle 146
Tay Lady 49
Tean 94, 95
Tern 56
Tessa 138, 139
The Londoner 24
The Mew .101
Thraki II 77
Thurstaston .60
Torbay Prince 49, 76
Totnes Castle 101
Totnes Princess 76
Tri Star 93
Tudor Prince 76, 96
Tuxedo Princess 128
Uganda 155
Ulster Lady .49
Ulster Monarch 45, 47, 48
Ulster Prince (1937) 40/41
Ulster Prince (1967) 39, 50
Ulster Queen 39, 50
Umanak 79
Upton 60
Valon 143
Vecta 91, 120, 121
Venus 54
Victoria 62
Viking III 78
Viking V 77
Viking Victory 78
Vortigern 130, 131
Wakefield .148
Wallasey 62
Waverley 20, 21, 23, 25, 35, 74, 88/89,
. . . . .134, 155, 134, 152/153, 154
Waverley Organisation 10, 21, 34
Western Belle 57, 103
Western Lady 106
Westward Ho 91
Whippingham 123
Wingfield Castle 147
Woodchurch 58, 59, 73, 97, 98
Wyre Lady .14

Hugh Town, St. Marys, is the largest town in the Scilly Isles. This tranquil scene, photographed on the afternoon of 30th August 1956, shows the quayside with the then new *Scillonian* (2) alongside and the inter-island boats *Kittern* and *Tean* moored next to her. *Scillonian's* hull doors are open to facilitate the transfer of goods (not passengers) destined for the outer islands. Both of the two inter-island boats were of the class of 54ft RN heavy duty launches and were strong, timber-built vessels dating from 1944 and 1941 respectively and acquired by the IOSSC in 1949 and 1953. They held Class IIA passenger certificates for fifty passengers enabling them to sail throughout the year, maintaining the vital links between the outer islands and St. Marys. Passengers for the outer isles joined the inter-island launches at the quayside and not through the hull doors. In 1961, a third ex-Naval launch was acquired and was given the name *Gugh* in 1962. See also p.94 and 95.

Richard Danielson Collection